THE ANTI-WITCH

HAU
BOOKS

www.haubooks.com

THE ANTI-WITCH

Jeanne Favret-Saada

Translated by
Matthew Carey

Foreword by
Veena Das

Hau Books
Chicago

Désorceler © 2009 Éditions de l'Olivier, Paris
English translation © 2015 Jeanne Favret-Saada and Hᴀᴜ Books.
All images reproduced with the authorization of France Cartes SAS.
All rights reserved.

Cover and layout design: Sheehan Moore
Typesetting: Prepress Plus (www.prepressplus.in)

ISBN: 978-0-9905050-4-4
LCCN: 2014953503

Hᴀᴜ Books
Chicago Distribution Center
11030 S. Langley
Chicago, IL 60628
www.haubooks.com

Hᴀᴜ Books is marketed and distributed by The University of Chicago Press.
www.press.uchicago.edu

Printed in the United States of America on acid-free paper.

Contents

Editorial Note   vii
Foreword by Veena Das   ix
Acknowledgments   xvii

I.   PRELUDE   1

II. UNWITTING THERAPY   11
     The psychoanalyst, the anthropologist, and the native   11
     The words of witchcraft   14
         The agents of witchcraft   14
         The ontological properties of agents and their actions   15
     Narrating witchcraft   16
         Exemplary narratives   17
         Exhortatory narratives   21
     Theory and practice   27

III. BIRTH OF A THERAPY   29
     Comparison of exemplary narratives   30
     Bewitching and dewitching   33
     The agents of witchcraft   36
         Those who lack "force"   36
         Dewitchers   38
         Witches   38

Abnormal force   39
  Trajectories   39
  Origins   40
  Abilities   42

IV. "OH THE WITCH, THE FILTHY BITCH, YOUR
     NEIGHBOR…"   47
     The therapeutic frame   48
     Healing the unwitting   49
     Violence shifters   52
     The deck of cards as therapeutic journey   56
       Cards with fixed meanings   57
       Cards with free-floating meanings   58
     Proof by tarot   59
     Neutralizing the anxiety-inducing field   60
     Prescribing actions   61
     The therapist's voice as act of enfolding   62

     The tarot cards of Mademoiselle Lenormand   64

V.   THOSE LEFT BEHIND BY THE SYMBOLIC
     ORDER   81
     State sanctification of custom   82
     Passive resistance versus enthusiastic commitment   83
     Salvation in the form of feminine wiles   84
     Therapy as housework   86
     On not being an "individual producer"   88
     It's since I set up in my own name…   90
     A catch-up institution   93

VI. BEING AFFECTED   97

References   109

Index   113

Editorial note

The original title of this book in French is *Désorceler*, first published by Éditions de l'Olivier in 2009. The translator, Matthew Carey, has properly rendered the term *désorceler* into English as "dewitching" and the text remains consistent in the translation of this and related terms. In agreement with the author, however, Hau Books has chosen to title this first English translation of the book as *The anti-witch*, a less precise and technical translation, to be sure, but one memorable and capable of highlighting the book's focus on the strategies for counteracting witchcraft. *Traduttore, traditore.*

The editors would like to extend their thanks to Éditions de l'Oliver for their kind permission to translate this text, and to Jeanne Favret-Saada for her enthusiastic support for Hau's publishing projects. Reproductions of the tarot card images from *Les cartes du petit cartomancien* and *Le grand jeu de Mademoiselle Lenormand* are printed with the authorization of France Cartes SAS.

Foreword

The occasion of the English translation of Jeanne Favret-Saada's book *Désorceler* is an event inviting or inciting us to reflect on how anthropological knowledge is constituted in a mode that is quite different from the various turns that have punctuated our discipline. Readers familiar with her earlier two books on witchcraft, *Deadly words: Witchcraft in the Bocage* (1980) and *Corps pour corps: Enquête sur la sorcellerie dans le Bocage* (1981, with Josée Contreras), will be grateful to Favret-Saada for further elucidation of the order of witchcraft and of the "therapeutic process" in dewitching, and also for the erudition and grace of her writing. Matthew Carey's translation makes the book read more like an original written in English than a translation from the French—I would characterize the book as more a transfiguration than a translation, for it testifies to a great collaboration between author and translator. This is also a moment for reflection: does the picture of anthropological knowledge in this book challenge us to interrogate our own pictures of knowledge and ask where and how does thinking happen? What are the specific ways that anthropologists are knitted to the worlds they study and represent as they give shape to their experiences in what is euphemistically called "the field"?

Favret-Saada questions the contrasts between "us" and "them" not on grounds of abstraction but through concrete categories that have structured the division of intellectual labor with regard to our understanding of the occult. She shows how a division between folklore and Anglo-American anthropology comes to be reflected in the manner in which the order of witchcraft in Europe becomes assigned to a past and

African witchcraft practices to the present. In the first case, folklore as a method of retrieving something that has disappeared from the modern world led to obscuring the way such practices might have changed over a period of time. In the second case, the subject was defined to focus on witchcraft accusations but not on what it meant to be bewitched or what dewitching did for those who sought cure or relief from the state of being bewitched. As she says:

> In other words, what mattered, for these [i.e., Anglo-American] anthropologists, was not participation, but observation. They had in fact a rather narrow conception of it: their analysis of witchcraft was reduced to that of accusations because, they said, those were the only "facts" an ethnographer could "observe." For them, accusation was a type of "behavior." In fact, it was the principal form of behavior present in witchcraft (its archetypal action), as it was the only one that could empirically be proven to exist. The rest was little more than native error and imagination. (Let us note in passing that, for these authors, speaking is neither a behavior nor an act capable of being observed.) These anthropologists gave clear answers to one question and one question only, "In a given society, who accuses whom of witchcraft?" and disregarded almost all the others: How does one enter into the state of being bewitched? How does one escape from it? What are the ideas, experiences, and practices of the bewitched and of witches? (this volume, 99)

So the first notable achievement of this book is that it redefines the questions to be asked and thus radically changes our angle of vision. On the historical side it shows that when a systematic comparison is undertaken with historical texts (she takes up one text, the two volumes of Jules Lecœur's *Esquisses du Bocage Normand*, published in 1883 and 1887), elements that one might think have disappeared in the witchcraft complex might reappear or be rearranged. However, what we can retrieve from the archives are basically "exemplary narratives"—i.e., the kinds of stories that people might tell well-meaning outsiders and that correspond to retrospective reflections on events. Such accounts might also be told in the fieldwork situation but do not capture the swirling affects, the shifts in relations, the dynamic shifting of categories of good and evil that Favret-Saada's ethnography and her own participation as a client in the dewitching process brings alive through the sheer power of her descriptions. It is to these remarkable shifts in relationships that I turn. I am interested, particularly, in what these shifts tell us about the kind of violence that one might detect in the everyday to which therapeutic process of dewitching responds, first, by deflecting blame to the socially acceptable categories of who might bear the blame of bewitching, and, second, by encouraging a mode of self-making that produces individual sensibilities that are in accord with the structural requirements of the farm family.

*

One strand of Favret Saada's argument is that the forms of bewitching and dewitching she encountered during her fieldwork in the region are rooted in the property relations of farm families and the lines of fissure these created. It is also the case, though, that when some of her work became available to a larger public, many people identified with the diffused anxieties of having to deal with multiple misfortunes in their lives and asked for guidance on where to seek a cure. What Favret-Saada identifies in the therapeutic process is both bound to the context of farm families in the Bocage but also goes beyond this context to provide insights into the nature of everyday life itself. I was truly captivated by the fact that several examples from my own ethnographic work corresponded closely to her descriptions about relationships, or about the psychic life and vulnerability of power. Is there a way, then, in which the forms of life through which the human is expressed in one corner of the world might bear resonances to another form of life outside the frameworks of humanitarian ethics or practices of sympathetic reading? In the remainder of this brief foreword I would like to ask why the story of bewitching and dewitching in the Bocage might be of compelling interest to current debates on ethics, ontology, or modes of self-making.

First, what is it about farm families that bears this close relation to the order of witchcraft, generating the pairs bewitcher-bewitched and dewitcher-dewitched? Second, how and what does Favret-Saada's bold move to recast dewitching as "therapy" tell us about how subjects reluctant to take on the social expectations entailed in their respective positions are brought into alignment with the social? To respond with care, we would be wise to follow the path Favret-Saada lays out for us, for it is not theory against ethnography but theory as ethnography that achieves the marvelous feat of knitting these two aspects of our forms of life together.

In the Bocage, bewitching is a diagnosis, arrived at by an expert (a dewitcher) through careful consideration of a client's description of a set of diffused anxieties that result from a series of misfortunes affecting the productive and reproductive capacities of the head of a farm family. It is usually a friend or a neighbor who advises such a family to seek help from a dewitcher. In some cases the dewitcher might deduce that the misfortunes are not related to the actions of a witch. In others he or she might diagnose the problem as that of a spell cast by a witch and offer a series of techniques to get rid of the spell cast on the affected person, his family, and his farm. The bewitched is inevitably the male head of the farm, for bewitching primarily affects the legal person (in possession of those capabilities proper to an owner) and only secondarily, the psychological person as the private individual with biographical particulars. The witch, then, is someone who wants to take away the vital force necessary for survival from the owner as head of the farm family.

Interestingly, when one finally reaches the dewitcher (who could be using several techniques, including reading tarot cards) in order to diagnose what misfortunes await the farm and how to mitigate these by turning the spell back, the dewitcher uses techniques of speech to elicit the name of the suspect from the head of the farm and his wife. There is, however, much obfuscation present in the process. The names of family members are blocked the moment anyone comes close to mentioning them and suspicion slowly settles on a neighbor (defined broadly). With masterly precision Favret-Saada shows how the dewitcher uses a combination of strategies ranging from the readings of the tarot cards to the rapid deployment of her (the dewitcher's) voice that rises to a crescendo, bringing images before the mind that flash with the speed of advertisements. Through this work performed in the presence of the dewitcher and through other work performed in the house under her instructions, a shift in subjectivities is attempted that will ultimately make the head of the farm able to overcome the resistances that he has built toward doing the psychic work necessary to make him a proper head of the farm—not only legally, but in terms of his own psychic reality. What is it that is required of the head to truly embody his legal position—to come to terms with the psychic realization that this is the kind of person he must become? The legal regime of property requires that one becomes an individual producer, autonomous and with full rights of ownership, by "despoiling, eliminating, and expropriating one's immediate forebears, collateral kin, and even one's wife"—for claims of other men over the farm must be extinguished and women must be placed within a position of dependence within the farm economy. This violence, says Favret-Saada, is legal and culturally acceptable. Yet, not everyone has the psychological wherewithal to accomplish this task. Dewitching then becomes a form of therapy in which the dewitcher and the wife of the bewitched couple come to establish a subtle cooperation in altering the psychic reality of the reluctant farm head.

I will not give away the surprises that come one's way when reading the precise manner in which this is accomplished. However some features are worth mentioning outright: there is, for example, the "violence shifter," a subtle play with the reading of the tarot cards through which a channel is opened between the bewitched couple's wife and the imagination of evil that is sucking away the vital force of the farm; there is the pronouncement of the formula—"it worked"—that carries illocutionary force; the changes that come about in forms of sociality in which the farm head and his wife were initially enmeshed, notably with regard to the person suspected of doing the witchcraft; and the many small acts of protection that must be undertaken that are akin to housework and shift the balance between husband and wife in the play of power. In other words, there is a whole complex of techniques, material objects, the tenor of the voice, etc. that are brought together in the dewitching process and that produce real effects. In the shifting of the psychic reality the person becomes more than himself, as Mme. Flora—the tarot card reader with whom Favret-Saada worked—brings about a distinction between the client as the person he is and what he must become as he begins to embody the great principles of law, justice, and truth. Dewitching, as she puts it, is not just another technique of self-assertiveness; a certain legal, but very real, violence is necessary to produce a happy farmer.

Given the fact that concepts have not only an identity but also a ground, we might ask: to what extent are the practices of bewitching and dewitching tied to the farm family alone? There are several moments in the text at which Favret-Saada is unequivocal that these practices are grounded in the legal realities of the farm family, and that once the ubiquity of family farms as a unique mode of organizing production and reproduction disappeared, these practices too disappeared. Yet, it seems to me that braided in this voice is a related claim in which we could, perhaps, detect a profound depiction of the nature of social life and its relation to anthropological knowledge.

Consider that Favret-Saada's own psychic reality did not remain untouched by her fieldwork—there was no possibility of her being able to live in the Bocage, show an interest in witchcraft, and remain outside the order of witchcraft. Unlike, let us say, Evans-Pritchard's basic axiom— viz. that we know witchcraft does not exist, hence converting a supposed ontological error into a semiotic truth (material causation substituted by efficient causation)—Favret-Saada is not so sure of the ontological status of the whole complex. This uncertainty is not unlike the shadow of skepticism that falls on all such experiences in everyday life. She thus deepens our understanding of what "participation" means in the production of anthropological knowledge and how our own certainties are staked in the process of getting to know an other as a concrete being.

Favret-Saada's analysis resonates deeply with my own understanding of a common "family drama" in India: upon the death of a father, the ascension of the brother to the position of the head of a household incites a melancholic sense of the inevitable unfolding of a lethal conflict between brothers over property, succession, and the even the right to propitiate ancestral deities. The two great epics of the Hindus, the Ramayana and the Mahabharata, attest to the power of this originary conflict as a story enshrined in kinship that is tragic but inevitable; it provides a powerful commentary on the conditions under which the social is produced. Mme. Flora's tarot cards are, indeed, far removed from Krishna's chariot on the eve of the battle of Kurukshetra in the Bhagvad Gita, but Krishna's lesson to Arjuna—who hesitates to be the one who will kill his cousins and elders for the sake of the righteousness of his cause—resonates (despite the great difference in techniques) with the necessity of opening a channel to the experience of evil in Bocagite dewitching. The specific events through which we encounter the kinds of risks that could drive us to madness are different, to be sure, but this book forcefully reveals our common vulnerability—not only to an external world of powerful institutions that can and do inflict violence, but also to the terrifying realization that therapy itself might be a means for making us the instruments of that violence. This is perhaps why the people Favret-Saada worked with insisted on a distinction between de-witching and cure from both physical and psychic ailments.

The claims and theoretical implications that I am making on behalf of the book (if not the author), especially those that break from the context of the farm family, are subtle and hidden in the text. I am tempted to say that they are only discernible through traces here and there, so I must seek the author's forgiveness for giving them voice. But I must also thank her, for *The anti-witch* is nothing short of anthropological therapy—it keeps the dream of ethnography as theory alive in these troubled times.

VEENA DAS
Baltimore, November 2014

Acknowledgments

Several friends helped me to walk the final steps of this long journey. First among them is Arnaud Esquerre. It was he who encouraged me to publish this book and he never stopped asking me challenging questions. I wish also to thank him for his part in producing that rare beast: an intellectual friendship.

Giordana Charuty, Marie-Aimée Hélie-Lucas, Hélène Puiseux, and Christine Salomon had the kindness and patience to read through several versions of the manuscript. My analysis of the role of women in the dewitching process owes a great deal to the many and endless conversations I had with Paola Tabet.

For this remarkable translation, I should like, first of all, to thank Matthew Carey, whose translation quite literally recreates in English a text that has become as dear to me as the French original: all traduttori are traditori, except this one. Sean Dowdy made the whole process of revising the manuscript into a book a source of real pleasure. I am equally indebted to him, and to Veena Das for her profound understanding of the book. Finally, my sincere gratitude to Giovanni da Col, the editors, and staff at Hau; its existence (the website, the journal, the book series, and all its other incarnations) has given me great hope in the future of anthropology as theory.

Certain parts of this book gave rise to presentations for audiences of anthropologists and psychoanalysts. I should like to thank them one and all for their comments and questions.

I carried out fieldwork on witchcraft in Mayenne from 1969 to 1972, later publishing two books: *Les Mots, la mort, les sorts: La sorcellerie dans le Bocage*, published by Gallimard in 1977[1] and *Corps pour corps: Enquête sur la sorcellerie dans le Bocage*, coauthored with Josée Contreras and also published by Gallimard, in 1981.

Then from 1981 to 1987, Josée Contreras and I continued to work on my witchcraft material. Together we published five articles and I wrote five more on different aspects of the question that I had explored by myself.[2] This volume reworks elements of all of these ten texts, linking them together so as to offer a general theory of dewitching and to tease out the epistemological implications of this ethnography of bewitchment that I began forty years ago.

It will be clear from the outset to what extent Josée Contreras was integral both to our and my writings and reflections on witchcraft. She has my entire gratitude for these years of intellectual cooperation, for her kind authorization to draw freely on our earlier work, and not least for her close and critical reading of the text.

Our coauthored works were:

1983. "Comment produire de l'énergie avec deux jeux de cartes." *Bulletin d'Ethnomédecine* 24: 3–36.

1985. "L'embrayeur de violence." In *The Self and the Other: Collection Analytic Space*, edited by Josée Contreras, Jeanne Favret-Saada, Jacques Hochmann, Octave Mannoni, and François Roustang, 95–148. Paris: Denoël.

1985. "La thérapie sans le savoir." *Nouvelle Revue de psychanalyse* 31: 223–38. [See Chapter Two, this volume.]

---

1. Translated as *Deadly words: Witchcraft in the Bocage* (Cambridge University Press, 1980).
2. Some of these texts were published after our work on dewitching came to an end. And in fact, we published many more texts, as a result of participating in various conferences, collective volumes, and so forth. They add, however, nothing to the ten core texts.

1990. "Ah! La féline, la sale voisine…" L'incroyable et ses preuves, *Terrain* 14: 21–31.
[See Chapter Four, this volume.]

1991. "Le travail thérapeutique comme production domestique." *Nouvelles Questions féministes* 16–18: 149–67.

My individual publications were:

1988. "L'invention d'une thérapie: La sorcellerie bocaine, 1887–1970." *Le Débat* 40: 29-46. [See Chapter Three, this volume.]

1989. "La genèse du producteur individuel." In *Singularités: Les voies d'émergence individuelle. Textes pour Éric de Dampierre*, 485–96. Paris: Plon. [See Chapter Five, this volume.]

1989. "Unbewitching as therapy." *American Ethnologist* 16 (1): 40–56. Reprinted in 1991 under the title "Le désorcèlement comme thérapie." Mélanges, *Ethnologie française* 21 (2): 160–74. [See Chapter Five, this volume.]

1990. "Être affecté." *Gradhiva* 8: 3–9. [See Chapter Six, this volume.]

JEANNE FAVRET-SAADA

Chapter One

Prelude

Between 1969 and 1972, I conducted fieldwork in rural northwest France, protecting it from the media curiosity surrounding questions of sorcery by vaguely referring to it as the Western French *Bocage* [Hedgerow region]. During my fieldwork, I met many "dewitchers," but I only worked extensively with one of them, a woman I call Madame Flora, who dewitched through tarot reading and cartomancy. In contrast to her colleagues, she could not visit the farms of bewitched peasants as she was infirm, and so instead received petitioners in the dining room of her little cottage. Our relationship swiftly acquired a professional footing and though it grew increasingly complex over time, it remained strictly professional: she was the dewitcher and I the client. She knew, of course, that I was a researcher and she was quite unconcerned by the fact that I would transform my experiences into a book.

I first visited Madame Flora when I had been living in the region for nearly a year. Several bewitched people had by then come to confide in me and their accounts filled me with a scarcely controllable dread. For the core theme of witchcraft narratives, their basic material, is a struggle to the death between warring partners: bewitcher and bewitched, bewitcher and dewitcher. These struggles may well be merely metaphorical, but they almost invariably have very real effects, including death. And when people told me their stories, it was never because I was an ethnographer but because they thought that I, like they, was "caught up" in a "spell."

They were not, however, of one mind. Some people concluded that my ability to bear these narratives was testament to significant magical "force" and so I must be a dewitcher, which is what they needed. Other more observant or less immediately imperiled acquaintances recognized my fear and decided I must have been bewitched. When one former victim informed me that my symptoms, as well as the state of my car, could only mean that I had been bewitched and that he would book me an appointment with his dewitcher, Madame Flora, I was almost relieved.

And yet. . . . In our first session, Madame Flora asked me to name any enemies I might have made. But even though I did not believe that I was the object of a witching attack and did not believe that giving her the names would lead to any deaths, I could not bring myself to do so. Each time she struck the table with her cane and insisted I name them, my mind went as blank as the patient's on the analyst's couch, when she is asked to engage in free association. For several weeks, I tried to avoid doing so, until I accepted that dewitching required the same commitment as psychoanalysis. From that day, I began to talk about myself in quite different and mutually exclusive ways: on the one hand to my Parisian psychoanalyst and on the other to my Bocagite[1] dewitcher.

In between meetings, I thought of Madame Flora with a mix of fear (when I heard echoes of her voice reading the tarot cards) and affection or enthusiasm. I often spoke of her to my local interlocutors, though I harbored a nagging fear that they might want to consult her too and that she might drag them too far down the path of violence, however symbolic it might be. Two farmers did insist on seeing her, however, and I duly arranged a meeting. To my great surprise, Madame Flora insisted I stayed for the session. And to my equally great surprise, when I returned home I was able to remember how the session had unfolded as well as the meaning of particular cards, something that I had previously been unable to do. This time, the reading was not directed at me and I was not called upon to respond: it was this, I decided, that allowed me to remember what happened.

---

1. This is an Anglicization of the French adjective "*bocain*." –Trans.

Unfortunately, this turned out not to be the case. These clients introduced me to others, who also wanted to visit Madame Flora and once more I attended the sessions. But on those occasions when I was caught up in the sufferings of the victim or smitten by Madame Flora's poetic sallies, then the same amnesia wiped clean my memory of events. I could cope with the experience of these murky situations, but I could not bear the thought of giving up on the attempt to understand them. So I decided to bring along a tape recorder so as to have a representative sample of actual exchanges between dewitcher and bewitched.

I did not explicitly discuss the use of the tape recorder with Madame Flora. I was reluctant to ask her outright as I was sure she must refuse. How could a practicing witch allow herself to be reduced to the role of mere anthropological informant? So I put the bulky object inside a canvas bag that I then placed right on top of the green baize of the card table. It was an old Philips that made a constant buzzing noise and so though it could not be seen, it could clearly be heard. When the tapes needed changing, I had to find some pretext to leave the room. Madame Flora saw through it at once and half-angry, half-amused, she said, "Oh come on! You're not seriously going to put a tape recorder on me?" Then she added, generously, "Make sure my name's not in the book. I don't want the police knocking at my door."

Once I had delegated the task of remembering to the machine and entrusted it with this minimal ethnographic labor, I no longer had to worry about questions of retaining some semblance of rationality. I could always sit down to interpret the events at some later date.

*

In 1981, after the publication of *Corps pour corps*, Josée Contreras and I sat down to write a chronological account of my meetings with Madame Flora's clients, their case histories, and our collective sessions. We thought that a simple narrative structure would make the dewitching process and its effects on clients accessible to the reader. And so together we reopened the bundle of documentation I had brought back from the Bocage: the recordings themselves (which captured the atmosphere of our sessions and the dewitcher's use of her voice), as well as a thousand pages of transcriptions and my field journal, which mentioned both the sessions with Madame Flora and my interviews with clients at their homes.

As we worked our way through this material, it seemed to slip increasingly through our fingers. Everything that could be said about a session, had already been said in *Corps pour corps*. The cases presented by the bewitched families were all unbearably similar and Madame Flora's patter seemed to be little more than random assertions and repetitions. Nor could we try to flesh out my notebooks. The entire period I had worked alongside Madame Flora, I had been under a sort of spell, a combination of fascination and naïveté, concerning her activities (which is doubtless the reason why she let me attend so many sessions and gather so much material). I had failed to develop the slightest understanding of her practice or cover any intellectual ground over the course of the dewitching. At the time, however, I was perfectly unaware of this and quite convinced that I had grasped the essential elements—I even went so far as to publicly announce my understanding in *Deadly words: Witchcraft in the Bocage* (1980), my second book on dewitching.

As we could not pursue a narrative approach, we had to rely on good, old-fashioned textual analysis of the sessions. We broke this mass of speech down into a series of short sequences that cropped up time and time again: the opening exchanges, dealing the cards, reading them, as well as the various digressions that Madame Flora built into the process, her accounts of other cases, and her discussions with clients about different decisions or actions to undertake, forms of protection, and references to her other witching activities. Next, we focused on those passages concerning the shuffling, dealing, and interpretation of cards, with a different file for each element. For instance, at what point during which séance and with regard to which subject does the dewitcher say what upon seeing a king of spades? Or a ten of hearts? Or a jack of diamonds? Which cards does she just mention in passing? And does she not mention some cards at all? And so forth? And we did the same for her two decorative nineteenth-century sets, which she alternated between depending on the circumstances. In short, we compiled a dictionary of interpretations and their precise contexts of utterance.

By the end of this meticulous inventory, Josée Contreras had spotted a recurrent anomaly in Madame Flora's interpretations. As a general rule, two particular cards represent the female protagonists of a case of

witchcraft: the wife of the bewitched couple and the wife of the bewitching couple. But in certain, very particular contexts, Madame Flora
systematically inverted their meanings.[2] Though I had never previously
noticed this technique, I immediately recognized its importance, dub-
bing it the "violence shifter" in an act of homage to Roman Jakobson.
This acted as a catalyst for subsequent realizations regarding Madame
Flora's way of practicing witchcraft, which quickly became clear to us.
This, in turn, allowed me to understand the practice of other witch-me-
diums I had encountered or had recounted to me.

*

Thus far, I have sketched out the different stages of my work on witchcraft: the fieldwork from 1969 to 1972,[3] the publication of *Deadly words*
in 1980 and of *Corps pour corps* with Josée Contreras in 1981; the analysis
of the material presented here over the next few months. This process
came to a close in 1987; all subsequent articles were reworkings of un-
published fragments.

I had stayed in touch with a number of people from the Bocage, especially the younger ones who had moved to Paris. And insofar as one
can rely on such fragile evidence, it seemed to me that the practice of
witchcraft continued largely unchanged. The region had, of course, been
affected by the wider social and mental changes occurring among the
peasantry, but things seemed to change at a leisurely pace. Subsequently,
an extended bout of illness left me thirsting for new questions to explore
and I put the topic to one side.

Now, however, as I prepare to publish *The anti-witch*, I feel I ought
to state clearly that, in my opinion, the type of witchcraft that I experienced in the Bocage no longer exists in its then form, if indeed it exists
at all.[4] For it was, as we shall see in Chapter 6, intimately tied up with

---

2. This process is analyzed further in Chapter 4.
3. In fact, I continued to live part-time in the Bocage until 1975 and though
   my fieldwork had come to an end, the conversations about witchcraft obviously did not.
4. Answers to these simple questions would have required several months of
   fieldwork.

a certain type of social fabric that has largely unraveled, especially over the last twenty years. For instance, many villages now house significant numbers of urban newcomers with no connection to the land (e.g., civil servants and pensioners, some of them British), and when the hamlets are not entirely abandoned, there is often only one farming family left. This massive social transformation can hardly have left a symbolic practice like witchcraft unchanged, as it is wholly dependent on contact with real people. I insist, however, that the form of sorcery discussed in *Deadly words* and *Corps pour corps,* and then analyzed more fully here is still of interest. All social and symbolic forms, extant or extinct, are legitimate objects of analysis insofar as they provide fodder for future comparison.

For more than a century, anthropologists have abused the gnomic present,[5] that uncertain time of actions neither past nor future, of general truths, proverbs, and theorems—an atemporal time, in short. This is often referred to, in anthropological circles, as the "ethnographic present" and its rhetorical use has been much criticized, though this criticism has not proved fatal (cf. Clifford and Marcus 1986). It allows so-called "primitive" or "traditional" societies to appear to float timelessly in a space made-up of first principles. And it makes fieldwork seem like some Arthurian act: an intrepid young man, armed only with the poor amulets of academia, abandons his *Umwelt* and plunges headlong into the society of one of the First Peoples, bringing back teachings to be transmitted to his own people. In contrast, I, as must be clear, harbor no illusions about an unchanging Bocagite society that I was lucky enough to encounter during my fieldwork. And so, I can allow myself the liberty of employing the historical present. This should be seen for what it is: a simple rhetorical device used to bring the chosen material closer to the reader.

*

During the period from 1969 to 1972, a large part of the local population (45 percent) still lived and worked on family concerns engaged in mixed farming, with both classic polyculture (meadows, cereal crops, fodder crops, and cider apples) and stock-rearing (dairy cattle, bullocks, calves, and swine). Of course, the modernization of agricultural practice had

---

5.   From *gnomos,* sentence.

already left its mark: tiny peasant smallholdings were already vanishingly rare and polyculture was gradually giving way to exclusive stock-rearing. Most farmers only owned a part of the land they worked and rented the rest, often from local gentry. Traditional inheritance practices in the area are normally described by lawyers as "egalitarian," which simply means that they did not enshrine any explicit forms of inequality: firstborn sons have no special privileges. In practice, however, some heirs are less equal than others, as women are systematically deprived of a significant part of their inheritance and the son who takes over from the parents (locally referred to as a "*reprenant*") does considerably better than his brothers. As the father's strength wanes, he gradually hands over the daily management of the land to the "reprenant" and sells him his tools and stock, thereby ensuring his own financial independence and allowing him to retire to the village.

Farms are inhabited by nuclear families composed of a couple and unmarried children. Once they reach the age of sixteen, young people who are not in education are expected to work on the farm for free for a decade or so, after which they are endowed with a lump sum allowing them to marry and set themselves up somewhere on a place of their own. Parents establish and endow the firstborn and then calculate transfers to younger children on this basis. This still leaves room, though, for countless minor adjustments and manipulations as parents tend to incorporate numerous objectively unassessable criteria, such as the cost of education or illness, numbers of years of free labor, et cetera. The way in which these *inter vivos* transfers and subsequent inheritance are calculated is a source of endless petty jealousies and even forms of hatred between siblings, especially brothers. Women's inheritance is calculated even more opaquely, unless they marry a farmer who insists they be given equal treatment.

Farms are typically scattered across the landscape or gathered in tiny hamlets with two or three families apiece. The villages, which are called "*bourgs*" (i.e., towns), house retired farmers, craftsmen, shopkeepers, and a few minor civil servants (postmen, teachers, and perhaps a doctor), collectively referred to as the "bourgeois." The rather loose urban fabric contains a more sizeable town every thirty miles or so, as well as the county town.

During the week, farmers are isolated. They leave the farm on rare occasions for professional reasons, and they pay visits to neighbors with whom they are friendly, in business or cooperation (it is worth pointing out that the term "neighbor" has a large degree of semantic elasticity in the area and is often contradicted by geography). On Sunday mornings, families visit the "bourg," first attending mass and then splitting up so the men can play cards in the local café while the women shop and children play on the square. In the early afternoon, farmers call in on relatives and friends, before going home to see to their animals.

In such a setting, social relations are such a blessing that one has to think twice before breaking them off. The regular triggers of family conflict are neutralized as much as possible and neighborly and cooperative relations are strictly regimented. As a general rule, open aggression is taboo: violent children are swiftly declared insane and sent to the local psychiatric institute; a man is only permitted to fight when drunk; and there is simply no question of a woman doing so.

Local inhabitants are politically and religiously conservative. All the farmers are baptized, confirmed, and buried at the church, and most attend Sunday mass. They are, however, anticlerical Catholics, who dismiss most priests as "faithless": "faithless" in that they have renounced the traditional faith and brutally imposed the "absurd" liturgical innovations of the second Vatican council; "faithless" in that they deny the reality of local healing saints and the superior "force" of the local Virgin and most recently canonized local saint (Thérèse de Lisieux); and finally "faithless" in their refusal to bless the farms of people convinced they have been bewitched. These faithless priests wear secular dress, drop into town in their little cars, and condemn all forms of superstition (going so far as to send the bewitched to psychiatric institutes), preaching the evils of drugs (which nobody would ever think to take), and advocating "enlightened faith." Whatever their social origins, they are seen as embodying urban values and the Enlightenment, along with the teacher and the doctor. True believers, faithful priests, in contrast (and a handful still remain), are necessarily born on a farm and are at their ease with peasants. They wear a well-darned cassock, walk about town reading a Latin breviary, agree to chant the *Dies Irae* at funerals, hold their drink when visiting, venerate local saints, and, last of all, agree to bless the bewitched and their chattel.

When a farm and its inhabitants are struck by some misfortune, one of the possible responses is witchcraft. At least in private, people regularly explain a particular class of misfortune in terms of witchcraft—those that strike a farm again and again without apparent reason: people or animals might fall sterile, sicken, or die; cows miscarry or dry up, vegetables rot or wither, stables burn down or collapse, machines stop working, and sales fall through or go badly. And when the farmers go to see specialists, such as mechanics, doctors, or vets, they declare themselves equally baffled.

These misfortunes are thought to testify to the head of the family's, the farmer's, loss of "force." It is only ever to him that the ritual declaration of potential witchcraft is made ("Perhaps somebody's out to get you") and it is he who is described as bewitched, even if personally he is fine. Cows, beets, tractors, children, pigsties, wives, and gardens are never bewitched in their own right, but by virtue of their connection to the head of the family, because they are his crops, his stock, his machines, his family. In short, his chattel. The bewitching primarily affects the legal person (in possession of those capacities proper to an owner) and only secondarily the psychological person (the private individual with his biographical particularities, personal traumas, and intrapsychic conflicts).

When a farmer is struck by repeated misfortune, people assume that "a witch is 'drawing away' [*rattirer*] his force." (In all likelihood, nobody in the region actually cast spells on anybody else, which does not of course prevent people from being affected by them.) The witch is also thought to be a head of a family / a farmer: somebody close but not a family member, who wants to capture the victim's everyday or vital "force"—i.e., his capacity for production, reproduction, and survival. The witch, meanwhile, is seen as endowed with an "abnormal force" for evil that can be exercised either through the practice of specific rituals or through everyday channels of communication, like the gaze, speech, or touch. As the witch's "abnormal force" feeds off the victim's force, it transforms the two farms into communicating vessels: one fills up with wealth, health, and life while the other is drained to ruin or death.

Any contact with the witch or his family can have terrible consequences and so the victim is forced to call upon the services of a "dewitcher," also possessed of "abnormal force." Dewitchers strive to keep their activity secret to avoid being legally charged with fraud or quackery. They often practice a "front" profession in either agriculture or as a craftsman. Each dewitcher has his or her own techniques and ways of talking and performing that may be honed through years of solitary practice or inspired by the person who initiated them and by whatever "books" may have fallen into their hands. When a farmer struck by misfortune calls upon the dewitcher, the latter deploys his force in a spectacular ritual designed to neutralize the witch's force and simultaneously allow the victim to recover his bioeconomic capital: health, fecundity, and fertility. That at least is the idea. As we shall see, however, Josée Contreras' and my analysis of the data collected during my stay led us to conclude that the dewitcher's work is primarily one of collective family therapy for the labor force of a farm.

Chapter Two

Unwitting therapy

THE PSYCHOANALYST, THE ANTHROPOLOGIST, AND THE NATIVE

Any practice designed to prevent the repetition of certain actions or states in a patient—i.e., any *therapeutic* practice—relies on a form of discourse that simultaneously defines and justifies its modus operandi. And perhaps this discourse can be used to examine the way in which the therapy works. Each form of therapy, in any case, claims to be able to do both, even though it denies the possibility that its competitors might do the same. Some therapists do recognize that one cannot simultaneously speak or act and be aware of everything one is saying or doing, but they fail to apply this recognition to the theory that underlies their practice.

Anthropologists, meanwhile, freely admit that a series of ritual acts can have immediate and spontaneous therapeutic effects for participants. Since Lévi-Strauss' famous text on symbolic efficacy ([1949] 1963a, cf. 1958) much work has underlined the therapeutic effectiveness of different kinds of ritual practitioners: Haitian spirit-possession specialists can indeed heal, as can their Mexican and Puerto Rican peers, African or American witch doctors, and Siberian or Thai shamans.[1] And here I

---

1. Few scholars have endeavored to describe exactly what it is that healers heal or to explain exactly how the healing process is supposed to work. I refer

suggest that the dewitchers of Western France should be thought of as therapists in much the same way.

No psychoanalyst has ever contested my right to use such terms to discuss dewitching, though they do insist that while it may have therapeutic effects, it is necessarily an inferior sort of cure, as it relies on techniques of suggestion.

My Bocagite informants, meanwhile, were they invited to take part in the debate, would doubtless lump psychoanalysts and anthropologists together: why should one describe ritual effects as "therapeutic" or label the immediate resolution of the suffering of bewitchment "a cure"? For they are quite clear that there exists a sharp distinction between physical and psychological ailments on the one hand and bewitching on the other, with the latter being characterized by long-term and catastrophic repetition of disasters affecting widely different aspects of a family farm— from people or animals falling sick to farm machinery breaking down, by way of poor harvests or unsuccessful sales—in short, anything that might affect the farm's productive or reproductive potential. Bewitching does not correspond to a particular form of illness and the specialist who deals with the problem is not a therapist, nor even a healer.

Dewitchers would be equally startled to hear themselves spoken of in such terms. Even those who engage in both dewitching and healing practices carefully distinguish between the two. When dewitching, practitioners neither examine their "patients" nor attend to their bodies with plants, concoctions, or prayers. They do not think of themselves as doctors, and much less as psychiatrists, psychologists, or psychoanalysts. Indeed, the last two classes of specialists, who claim to heal with words alone, are considered at best liars (who refuse to recognize that, in fact, they "do" something) and at worst incompetent (for if they really do nothing, how can they bring an end to such cycles?). Dewitchers would only claim to be "doing" something: words are only used for pronouncing set phrases, not for proposing interpretations or stringing together chains of free association. For instance, a dewitcher might stick a thousand pins in a beef heart while ritually defying the witch: if the dewitcher's force is "strong enough" (*fort assez*) then "it works" (*ça y fait*) and the cycle of repetition is brought to a close.

---

the reader to the works by A. Harwood, Gananath Obeyesekere, Stanley Tambiah, and A. Young in the reference list.

In short, all my informants, dewitchers and lay folk alike, would contest my use of therapeutic language to describe dewitching. Of course, I have my reasons for doing so, but local understandings are nonetheless important and we must first endeavor to understand how my informants conceptualize and discuss acts of bewitchment, the dewitcher's role, actions, and potential effects, as well as her modus operandi.

Readers who have themselves undergone talking cures might be surprised by the lack of any clear distinction between the understandings of the bewitched and those of the dewitchers, as if patient and practitioner were both equally authorized to opine on the practice.

Talking cures that emerge from highly literate social milieux base their credibility on an enormous theoretical corpus and considerable conceptual refinement, both of which practitioners are expected to augment and which they may spend a lifetime studying, by reading or participating in conferences, seminars, and working groups. It is, for the most part, these professionals (and they alone) who can speak with authority on therapeutic practice. Patients can only internalize and reproduce the discourse as if they were themselves therapists or, better yet, actually become therapists. In the meantime, they may share stories of quasi-miraculous interpretations with one another, or pose questions, or make demands regarding the cure. This, though, is not the discourse of a therapist, but that of a patient—enthusiastic neophytes, people who resist the therapy, or are unfamiliar with it. With few exceptions (the occasional schizophrenic genius or anorexic prodigy), the users' perspective is summarily "disqualified" or dismissed by both therapists and patients alike. Trainee therapists are equally caught up in the notion that their reflections are necessarily incorrect or insufficient: perhaps they have misread their theory, twisted their therapist's words or traduced his intentions, projected their own personal issues onto clinical cases. . . . In sum, talking cures endow therapists with two indissociable qualities (knowledge and know-how), while patients are endowed with the corresponding faults.

In the Bocage, knowledge of dewitching and ritual know-how are completely decoupled. Dewitchers learn on an ad hoc basis, often through contact with an older practitioner who recognized their "gift" and "hands down the secret" of dewitching before retiring. They absolutely do not seek to increase their knowledge; "everyone has their own secret technique," as they put it. Dewitchers are possessed of a "secret" (ritual know-how) and a certain amount of "force" (a capacity for action or doing). Neither of these gives them access to a doctrine of knowledge that is, by its very essence, inaccessible or impossible to communicate to the uninitiated. Indeed, the bewitched listen to dewitchers recount the derring-do of their previous magical combats in just the same terms as they tell similar stories they have heard. They see them test their mettle (their "force"), however, in the ritual act, and it is on this act that their credibility hinges. The statement "it's worked" says everything that needs saying. As the action remains firmly rooted in the realm of "doing," there is no call for theoretical justification or general commentary. This does not, of course, imply that dewitching (and witchcraft more generally) has no corresponding cognitive framework, but it is quite different in nature to that of more intellectual forms of therapy. Witching discourse can be situated on two levels: on a straightforward level, we find a limited number of terms and their rules of use; and on a more complex level, we find a wider range of narratives and their rules of enunciation. Let us not forget, however, that only dewitchers and the bewitched discuss witchcraft, and only in very restricted contexts; suspected witches do not mention the topic or, if questioned, they state that they do not believe in it and simply dismiss or "disqualify" their accusers' claims.

THE WORDS OF WITCHCRAFT

Let us first focus on Bocagite witchcraft terminology. Some terms, which concern the different agents (witch and dewitcher), are known to locals but rarely appear in speech, while other terms related to the ontological properties of these agents and their actions are both known and present in speech, although their semantic content is invariably vague.

The agents of witchcraft

Even when a bewitched person is discussing his condition with a close friend or relative whom he trusts implicitly, he never mentions the terms "witch" or "dewitcher"; nor does he refer to their surnames or exactly where they live. Instead, he may have recourse to certain vague or euphemistic set expressions. A witch may be referred to as "the one who did me" (*celui qui me l'a fait*), the "piece of shit" (*la saloperie*), or "him there" (*l'autre*)—all of which are quite unequivocal regarding the witch's guilt. The dewitcher, meanwhile, may be "the expert in that business" (*un qui est fort pour ça*), "that woman who does what needs doing" (*la femme qui fait ce qu'elle a à faire*), or "that bloke from Cossé-le-Vivien" (*l'homme de Cossé-le-Vivien*), when the dewitcher does indeed live in the parish of Cossé-le-Vivien, but in a different village fifteen miles away. Such acts of deliberate obfuscation are the result of speakers' self-censorship, which they exercise because they feel caught in a dual power struggle (both magical and political).

On the one hand, people believe that witches have the supernatural ability to hear from afar. The bewitched and their confidants are thus forced to keep things vague, otherwise the witch might realize that he has been identified and think to himself: "if so-and-so speaks of bewitchment or names me, that must mean he has consulted a dewitcher, and I will be attacked." Faced with this threat, the witch may redouble his trickery (*tours de force*) to eliminate his victim while there is still time. For the same reasons, the bewitched person avoids the word "dewitcher," as well as any specific place or personal names that might expose his champion to attack.

And on the other hand, clear and straightforward language might afford a passing "nonbeliever" (in witchcraft—such as a local positivist) the possibility of denouncing the dewitcher to the local police, as well as of publicly decrying the victim for his credulity and backwardness. It is thus critical to prevent just such a person from understanding. These terms that can only be used so long as they fail to refer to a particular person might almost be described as paradoxical. They emerge from an understanding of the world that attaches supreme importance to acts, with speech being seen as an act with incalculable consequences. When one is caught up in a cycle of misfortune, one must necessarily discuss it with one's close friends and relatives, if only to dull the anxiety caused by repetition or seek some way out. And yet the omnipresent fear of speech acts forces speakers constantly to camouflage what they say.

The ontological properties of agents and their actions

Here, the terminology is no less imprecise, but the imprecision is not deliberate. Instead, it marks the presence of an unthinkable, inconceivable, and unrepresentable thought object. For instance, a witch may "seize hold of" (*prend*) or "play tricks" (*jouer des tours*) on you because he is strong (*fort*), but in what does his "force" consist? In what sense is it abnormal and irreducible to the productive and reproductive potential mentioned above. Locals cannot describe in detail either the nature or the modus operandi of such force; they can only indicate the channels through which it flows (speech, touch, gaze) and its end result: cycles of misfortune. Bewitching is the enactment of this inconceivable force. The dewitcher's force is equally resistant to definition or paraphrase and its principal quality is the capacity its holder possesses of being able "to do what he has to do"—viz. "to turn the bewitchment [this indefinable thought object] back on the witch."

For instance, a classic sign of bewitchment is the appearance of so-called "butter-marks" (*beurrées*) in a farmer's fields: milky looking fungal growths that appear on the grass. They indicate that a witch has visited at night and "touched" one of the animals in the stable, plucking a few tail hairs and reciting a spell. In the morning, the cow produces only thin milk that cannot be sold—the milk's fat has drained into the butter-mark. The bewitched farmer may then burn the fungal growths with petrol, while throwing a handful of metal shrapnel into the flames. "It's hard to burn," I was told, "but boy can that bastard feel it." With this, the farmer drives the fat back into his cow's udder and punishes the witch by metaphorically sticking him with burning nails—without ever taking the risk of explicitly stating anything.

There are, then, two obstacles in the way of witchcraft terminology directly referring to anything: the speaker's (*signifiant*) fear and the indeterminacy of that which is spoken (*signifié*). What we can unequivocally state, however, is that the inhabitants of the Bocage credit 1) the existence of a mysterious "force" that can affect people (why, though, are some people endowed with this force while others have none?) and that moves along ordinary channels of human communication; and 2) that the system is arranged such that those possessed of this force (witches and dewitchers) can either attack or protect those who have no such arms (the bewitched).

NARRATING WITCHCRAFT

The terminology discussed above features in the narratives that describe the different possible trajectories of this force between the different protagonists of a bewitchment. There are two kinds of oral narrative, each of which is subject to specific rules of utterance: I shall call them "exemplary" and "exhortatory."[2]

Exemplary narratives

This is the most common and most striking type of narrative. It describes in straightforward terms the invariable structure of a bewitchment: a family of honest and hard-working farmers, who are on friendly terms with their neighbors, are suddenly struck by a series of increasingly severe misfortunes, which may affect any aspect of the family business. Stunned, terrified, and despairing, the family wonders what can possibly be going on. All in vain. Each misfortune, taken individually, resists rational analysis, and this is a fortiori so when they are taken as a series. In some cases, these people have never even heard of witchcraft, in others, they don't believe in it, and in others still it hadn't crossed their minds that a witch might be at work. Someone close to them, perhaps a friend, a relative, or a neighbor, who has previously suffered from witchcraft, watches their steady ruin. At last, he speaks directly to the head of the family and pronounces the consecrated phrase: "Perhaps somebody's out to get you." The victim is startled into understanding, accepts the "revelator's" (*annonciateur*) arguments and finally agrees to visit his former dewitcher.

If the dewitcher confirms the diagnosis then he will undertake the dewitching in the presence of the afflicted family and the afflicted family alone. This exemplary narrative misses out the act and process of identifying the witch, but invariably describes the ritual used to defeat him: boil a beef heart, stick it with a thousand pins, and solemnly challenge the witch; or alternatively, fry some kosher salt in a red-hot skillet and . . .

All the different versions of the narrative insist that these ritual acts have an immediate effect on the witch, who is always situated at some distance from the farm where the dewitcher is at work. For instance:

---

2.   In the original text, I used the terms "typical" and "incomplete" to describe these different types of narrative. I now prefer, however, to stress their differing pragmatic aims: the term "exemplary" refers to the classical *exemplum*, a narrative designed to convince a listener by example, while "exhortatory" refers to the speaker's exhorting of the listener actively to follow through with a dewitching.

"Izé's wife fried the salt in the skillet and him there he began to hop back and forth from one leg to the other, hopping, hopping with pain!" The narrator neglects to mention how he knew this, as the salt and the witch were not in the same place. "As soon as the bloke from Mortain had stuck the needles in, then him there he runs up screaming, 'Ow!' 'Ow!' with the pain, he couldn't bear it." And the narrator never says how the witch was identified, but the ritual always confirms that the accused was also the guilty party. What is more, the dewitcher never knows the witch as he lives far from his clients and is ignorant of their personal history, circumstances, and networks.

The narrative ends with the witch's ruin, as he in turn is struck by a series of incomprehensible, repetitive misfortunes, similar to those that befell the initial victim. It is so obvious that the dewitched family recovers its former productive and reproductive capacity (health, fertility of the animals, and soil) that it sometimes literally goes without saying.

The dewitcher's work, then, is limited to punishing the witch in absentia via a ritual act that has an instantaneous effect on the culprit. There is nothing in the exemplary narrative to suggest that the dewitching might be seen as a "cure" or to allow one to infer that the dewitcher's actions were in some sense therapeutic for the family. The bewitched family plays no active part in the ritual process and their silent presence is barely mentioned. All the attention is focused on the titanic struggle between the dewitcher and the invisible witch, as the former trembles, sweats, falls, and sometimes cries out: "It's his body or mine. Either he's had it or I have!" And the narrator never suggests that the bewitched family derived any therapeutic benefit from the whole business. The cycle of misfortune is broken, but personally they have made no progress, covered no ground, they simply move from being passive victims to victors by proxy. It is as if their only role in the whole affair was to appeal to a dewitcher, and even that on the advice of the "revelator."

One might easily conclude that there is little more to this than a local tendency to narrate the impossible: "At the precise moment when, at farm A, the dewitcher undertakes the ritual, at farm B, the witch receives a sharp somatic shock that sets in motion a cycle of disasters." Believing in dewitching amounts to asserting this sort of proposition. Indeed, exemplary narratives contain this sort of proposition and, in fact, only this sort of proposition. But before we roundly declare that it is this and this alone that the peasants of the Bocage believe, and thus and thus alone that they represent dewitching, it is worth turning our attention to the pragmatic context of enunciation and asking who tells these narratives to whom and to what end.

Supposed witches do not tell witching stories as they claim not to believe in the phenomenon. "Nonbelievers," whose only aim is to ridicule the gullible, restrict themselves to stories of charlatans pulling the wool over the eyes of imbeciles. It follows that the only people who tell such exemplary tales are "believers"—either people who have been bewitched or those close to them. These narrators can be divided into two distinct groups: those possessed of "force" and those who have none.

When an ordinary, "forceless" victim of witchcraft tells such a tale, it never describes his own experience. For even if he has been victorious, the former victim is always afraid of reinvoking the witch's force by reactivating the channels of speech, of rekindling the evil, and being caught up in it once more. In short, once a witching episode is over, then it is dead and buried for the victims in the affair, definitively excluded from their discursive field. The utterance, "I was bewitched on such and such a date and thanks to this particular dewitcher, I am rid of the evil" is as impossible to say as the utterance "I am dead" at the end of an autobiographical account. As such, victims of witchcraft can only recount the travails of others: travails of which they can only have indirect knowledge. They are, then, in an identical narrative position to that of "believers" who have never been bewitched.

All members of this class of narrators (those without "force") claim to be telling true stories, not fictions. They happily concede that their sources are indirect, but they insist they are trustworthy. Some claim to be certain of the truth of their tale because at the time of events they were close to the victims, who were friends, relatives, or neighbors. In many instances, though, they have never openly discussed the matter with those concerned, never been directly told what happened, and no narrator ever claims to have witnessed the struggle between witch and dewitcher. Instead, they spend months observing and inferring[3] and ultimately they feel authorized to promulgate their version (yet another exemplary narrative) as they have a wealth of supporting evidence to

---

3.   Drawing on the large stock of existing tales to which they have access.

buttress their claims. Other narrators have never even met the heroes of
their tale, but they believe it to be true as they can describe the nature of
the relationship between the different links in the narrative chain lead-
ing from the first narrator to themselves.

When a narrator is possessed of "force," then he is necessarily a dewitcher, as witch is not a possible narratory identity. Only a dewitcher
can tell his own story, as he has nothing to fear from a witch who has
already proved himself to be "weaker" than he is, whom he has already
vanquished in magic combat. He can then unite the subject of enunciation (the narrator) and the subject of the statement (the central character) in one narrative.[4]

These tales of witchcraft, reduced to their simplest expression as a
demonstration of the efficacy of magic, are—like all tales—made to be
told and retold. But not to just anyone.

They are typically told to other known "believers"—i.e., to people
who are equally convinced that they refer to real-life experiences—people who share the narrator's ingenuity regarding the various storytelling
techniques deployed in the narrative. The tale does not raise questions; it
simply commands fascination. If listeners decide to speak up, it will only
be to add to the tale with tales of their own, designed to command the
same fascination and maintain the same ingenuity. They may also, however, be told to people whose position regarding witchcraft is unknown
to the narrator: for instance, if an ambiguous conversation is struck up
with a friendly interlocutor (such as an anthropologist) who does not
declare their skepticism outright, as an "unbeliever" would invariably
have done. The interlocutor's position is unknown. So one trots out a
particularly provocative exemplary narrative. Is the other person capable
of listening to the end? Does he seem impressed and so remain silent
until the tale is told? Does he raise basic objections regarding its reality?
Does he tarry on minor details? One's interlocutor's reactions allow one
quickly to ascertain whom one is dealing with: if no objections are raised,
he is a clandestine "believer"; if he cavils, a skeptic.

Though narrators of such tales claim to be telling true stories, their
aim is not to provide a close description of what happens during a dewitching and much less to reveal how dewitching works. Instead, the

---

4.   These terms are drawn from the work of Émile Benveniste. —Trans.

narrator aims simultaneously to assert the two central tenets of witching thought: "bewitchment is real" and "dewitching works."

Exhortatory narratives

What, though, when it "doesn't work"? Or doesn't work enough? Or doesn't work yet? When faced with total failure, or with relative or delayed success, witchcraft discourse offers another narrative genre—one that is always incomplete because the crisis is ongoing. Only those engaged in a process of dewitching can formulate exhortatory narratives.[5] The narrator always relates his own situation, but only to a specific interlocutor and for specific reasons. When this narrator is a dewitcher, then such tales may be told to new clients as an oblique means of imparting an understanding of the essential conditions of their salvation. When a bewitched person tells them, they are addressed to a new dewitcher, whom he exhorts to demonstrate a greater degree of force than his unsuccessful predecessor.[6] As the dewitcher needs to know precisely what his predecessor has already tried, these narratives contain a wealth of concrete information concerning the dewitching process.

The climactic scene of magical combat plays a relatively small role because the ritual had no decisive impact, but the preliminary labor and the ritual aftermath (which are barely mentioned in exemplary narratives) are discussed at length. What is more, these narratives contain numerous references to the complex and, at times, highly charged relationship that develops between dewitcher and client. Such relationships are evidently not restricted to one short ritual, nor are they reducible to a simple transaction between a producer and a consumer of a performance.

Once a dewitcher has met his clients, his first task is to settle on a diagnosis[7] by answering the following questions: Is this indicative of witchcraft? If so, how serious is it? Are the farmers in a "death-grip"? How many witches are involved? For how long have they been at work? What are their motives? It will take five or six nights of dedicated labor to answer these questions and reach a diagnosis.

---

5.   This explains the absence of dewitchers from ethnographic texts.
6.   I was told such tales when people mistook me for a dewitcher.
7.   Which, perhaps surprisingly, is not always positive.

First, the dewitcher undertakes a close inspection of the farm: the farmhouse itself, room by room; then the farm buildings (stables, sties, coops, barns), paying special attention to hearths and entryways; the fields; livestock, one-by-one; agricultural machinery; the car; and so on. At various stages, the inspection will be interrupted by moments of drama: the dewitcher may stagger or fall or appear to be struck by invisible blows. He gauges the enemy's "force" in his very body, folding over, righting himself, and providing a slightly stressed running commentary: "Oh! This one's [the witch] mean. I don't know if I've got the strength" or "You're bewitched from all sides; you're surrounded."

Next comes a long and tense interview, where the bewitched family are meant to "tell all" ("you've got to spill the lot, or he says he can't help"), draw up a chronological list of their misfortunes and for each event say who they saw around that time. Witches are invariably part of the victims' social circle[8]—people one knows from the village, to chat to, lend a hand, people who might drop by the farm. Only three categories of people are excluded. First, the immediate nuclear family, which is understood as a unitary, indivisible entity that necessarily stands together. Then, people who have no direct contact with the bewitched family—for the witch's force is conveyed by speech, gaze, and touch. And finally, those who have irregular contact with the family, as the witch must "work some evil every day."

During this process, several crucial points must be addressed, notably the run-up to the marriage (How did husband and wife choose one another? Were there any rivals?), the legal and financial situation when the farm was established (Did the farmer inherit from his father? Was the father still alive when this happened? How were matters settled with the brothers?), and the current situation (Is it carrying an excess of debt? To whom is the debt owed? The bank? Relatives? Private individuals? And how were and are relations with these different people?). This irrevocably alters the way the bewitched family thinks of their situation: as the dewitcher asks questions, they are forced to rethink whole swathes of their lives and relations, recalling forgotten episodes and making unexpected links. Little by little, the protagonists work their way toward

---

8.   This social circle, however, is not restricted to neighbors, as French ethnography often suggests.

a coherent and stable vision of the situation and direct their accusatory gaze toward one or two witches. As the family inspects the foundations of its communal existence, revealing them to an outsider, and unveils its jealously guarded financial secrets, it is drawn into an intimate relationship with the dewitcher.

Once the dewitcher has confirmed that they are bewitched and gauged the enemy's strength, he states whether or not he will try to drive back the bewitchment (*rabattre le sort*), depending on whether he considers he has sufficient "force." If he agrees to try, then it is up to the bewitched family whether or not they wish to proceed, depending on how they feel about fighting evil with evil (*rendre le mal pour le mal*). They often hesitate, as it may run counter to their self-image. The bewitched normally think of themselves as good Christians, as people who want only what is best for others. How could anybody want to injure them when they are so good, so harmless? They may need months to come to a decision, during which time they wonder which is worse: bearing the responsibility for launching a magical attack or the worsening cycle of misfortune, which has not abated? They then return to the dewitcher, both to recount their more recent woes and to make up their mind about him. Is he a charlatan or real dewitcher? How far will he take them down the path of "doing harm"? The family may also send the "revelator" in their stead, usually on some flimsy pretext. His task is to assess whether the dewitcher is still honest and upright, ready to wield his "force" in defense of the innocent. The dewitching begins only once the dewitcher has their full confidence.

In exemplary narratives, the whole thing is over when the dewitcher's combat with the invisible witch is brought to a close with the words: "The woman who did you . . . she won't do you again." "Three days from now, she'll be brought low." Exhortatory narratives, in contrast, dwell on the aftermath of the ritual, when they all gather around the kitchen table with a jug of steaming coffee and a bottle of firewater. The bewitched family keeps on talking and the dewitcher, who has now completed his ritual labor, prescribes a series of urgent measures that should help, drawing on his experience of past cases. This extended narrative activity aims to drive home the idea that if the bewitched are to recover their productive and reproductive potential, they must take responsibility for certain things and alter their behavior in particular ways, otherwise nothing will change. Many narratives blame the failure of a dewitching ritual on the family's inability or refusal to implement fully the dewitcher's recommendations.

The main line of these recommendations is to implement a general shutdown (*tout clencher*)—i.e., to close all points of entry or egress.[9] Witching thought conceives of a farm and the family who works it as a single, unified surface exposed to magical attack. Two kinds of barrier can be used to protect this surface: normal material barriers, such as fences and locked doors or gates impede physical access to the farm, while invisible or hidden magical barriers, such as saintly medals, holy water, or salts ward off maleficent "force." Every aspect of the farm must be protected in every possible way. So a medal of Saint Benedict will be hung in the car, its bonnet sprinkled with holy water, and it will be locked and further parked in a locked garage. And its driver will pin an apotropaic sachet to his vest and fill his pockets with holy salts. Things that are difficult physically to shut off or lock down (e.g., fields and grazing livestock) can be "insulated" from attack (by walking a circle around it and scattering holy salts) or sealed off (by blocking any "openings"[10] with magical substances). These actions are renewed at specific junctures (supposedly inauspicious periods), such as key moments in the productive and reproductive cycle (before sowing crops or calving), and, more generally, whenever they are needed—for instance, if one has contact with a known or suspected witch.

In theory, all contact with witches must be avoided: "stay away from them"; "don't speak to them"; "don't touch them"; "refuse to shake their hands"; "don't touch anything they've touched."[11] Unavoidable contact must be neutralized. So, if a witch speaks to you and you have to reply,

---

9. This is necessary because the family cannot be certain that there was only one witch at work. If the cycle of misfortune continues, it means that at least one more witch is still on the prowl.

10. The term "opening" must here be understood both literally (animals' mouths, thresholds, beginnings of paths) and in a variety of metaphorical senses (ailing parts of beasts or men or the body of the bewitched as a whole).

11. Better yet, commit to flames anything they have touched—e.g., the bread they often fetch you from the baker's or a tool they may have borrowed and now return.

simply repeat his last words; if he looks at you, hold his gaze; and if he drops by your house, then "salt his ass" by sprinkling holy salts behind him. I could expatiate further on the innumerable recommendations proposed after the climactic ritual combat. Indeed, exhortatory narratives mention dozens of them and frequently dwell, not without a degree of self-satisfaction, on the perfection with which the program was carried out, implying that failure must then be attributed to the dewitcher's lack of "force."[12] The sheer number of such recommendations calls for a couple of comments.

Following so many new rules is tantamount to changing one's life—one's days now beat to the rhythm of ritual activity that can take up as much as several hours, and one's thoughts and conversations revolve around how to behave in such and such a situation. In short, the bewitched move from a position of passive and resigned victimhood to one of hyperactivity that involves training oneself to do the right thing at the right time.

These recommendations are presented as simple self-defense but they all contain a degree of aggression that is scarcely evoked but always present. Thus, the prayers addressed to the "God of Mercy" contain an explicit denunciation of witches and a call for their punishment on the grounds of *lex talionis* (an eye for an eye). Medals of Saint Benedict protect thresholds by dint of their "force," which can drive back the witch who might try to cross it or strike him such a blow that the message hits home. The bewitched can never remove their apotropaic sachets, which contain both protective elements (e.g., a chunk of a Paschal candle) and "sharp things that pierce." The supposed target of this metaphorical aggression may well be blithely unaware of the attacks, but the aggressor cannot but recognize his responsibility for them, at least partially, and this has a psychological effect.

In a region where nothing is normally "closed off" or "shut down" because theft and murder are vanishingly rare (the lowest rates in France), where animals graze in the open year round, farm buildings are protected only by the wind, and even houses are only symbolically closed (a key is

---

12. As we saw above, lists of such recommendations also feature in dewitchers' narratives, but here they serve to remind the bewitched family of the dangers of sloppiness of execution.

normally left in the derelict bakehouse if one is out), the erection of visible barriers is a marked affront to one's neighbors and friends—it implies that one sees them as potential evildoers. The avoidance and neutralization techniques are just as offensive. Overnight, friends, neighbors, or relatives may find themselves shut out in a thousand different ways.[13] The family no longer greets them, simply repeats their last words, cuts off all relations of cooperation or mutual help, stares at them until they lower their gaze, refuses them entry to the farm, and shuns an outstretched hand or brushes it aside with cryptic comments such as, "I'll touch your hands when they're clean." The setting up of everyday barriers amounts to a series of silent acts of aggression that speak louder than words—acts that (we can safely assume) modify radically not only the family's relations with its social circle but also the psychological stances of its members.

It takes a while to implement all these different measures and longer still to make sure that "it worked," that the witch's family and farm have been caught up in their own cycle of misfortune, while the bewitched family has broken free of theirs and completely recovered its productive and reproductive potential. The most obvious signs of bewitchment seem in most cases quickly to vanish after the pivotal moment of magical combat, but it takes several months to make sure that the dewitching worked (the time to run through a cultural cycle, see animals or people bring a pregnancy to term, for a financial year to come to an end, etc.). During this probational period, the bewitched must not only sedulously keep up their aggressive noncommunication but must also minutely observe the supposed witch and his family: they pounce upon and dissect the merest element of information, look out for the slightest sign of misfortune, and excitedly compare the miniscule changes that affect either family or farm. They also talk them over with their dewitcher. For the dewitcher's task is not done when the ritual combat comes to an end. He watches night and day for the "forces" that might threaten his clients or afflict his own body. He may turn up at the farm unannounced because he has "seen" the witch attempt a magical attack. In other words, months after the dramatic events that mark the end of exemplary narratives, the

---

13. Dewitchers normally avoid pointing the finger at anyone with whom the family is on overtly bad terms, so the witch elect cannot initially understand this change in behavior and feels himself unfairly maligned.

dewitcher is yet to be demobilized. And even when the crisis has been brought to a satisfactory conclusion, he remains the lifelong guarantor of the "normalcy" of his clients' family and farm and they will return to him at the slightest sign of "abnormality."

As we have seen, symbolic efficacy implies that messages travel along two channels: from dewitcher to bewitched and from bewitched to witch. The mediating role played by the bewitched family is capital. To drive the bewitchment back upon a witch with whom he has no direct contact, the dewitcher relies on his clients to make the witch understand that he is faced with an adversary who is also possessed of "force."

THEORY AND PRACTICE

Each aspect of witching discourse confirms the real-world efficacy of its metaphorical acts. Indeed, speakers deem it so potent that they avoid referring to particular witches; it goes so far beyond the limits of the thinkable that the ontological qualities and actions of people possessed of "force" are indefinable, or at least can only be defined negatively. There exists a particular narrative genre (which I have called "exemplary") that showcases the most impressive example of this efficacy. Even those tales that revolve around its failure still portray it as the only possible model.

In all contexts where "believers" feel free to speak of witchcraft, they clearly and unequivocally assert the real-world efficacy of ritual. As such, we can describe it as the theory or "credo" of the witchcraft believer— what one must assert if one claims to be a dewitcher or has recourse to one. And yet, this theory, which believers seem to find sufficient, helps us to understand precisely nothing in regard to the process of dewitching. In particular, it leaves open the question of how the cycle of misfortune shifts from one camp to the other.

Exhortatory narratives also proclaim the real-world efficacy of ritual, but what they show is something different: the existence of a relationship between dewitcher and bewitched that aims to drive these latter from their position of passive victimhood[14] by redirecting the violence toward an uninvolved third party. We might say that these elements are

---

14. And this is why I describe the relationship as therapeutic.

admitted without being overtly recognized: though they are omnipresent in narratives, they have no theoretical status, and sometimes they
don't even have a name. But their absence from the theory of dewitching
does not mean that they do not number among the representations or
mental objects proper to the practice.

So, in exemplary narratives, there is a theory of dewitching that masks
the means by which it achieves efficacy. And in exhortatory narratives we
find not only the same theory but also a series of representations that
reveal the way in which it achieves efficacy, but only insofar as they are
situated outside of the scope of theory. There is no contradiction between
representation and theory, but instead a contraction of the dewitching
process. This contraction endows the theory with what is, for locals, its
emblematic and necessary function: by not referring to it, they would
step outside the order of witchcraft and, in so doing, they would abandon
the necessary misrecognition of "what works."

CHAPTER THREE

Birth of a therapy

Taking its lead from popular understandings of the phenomenon, French ethnology has consistently portrayed contemporary peasant witchcraft in Europe as a coherent mass of ideas and practices handed down unchanged since time immemorial. Even the illustrious Lévi-Strauss declared it to have "limited adaptability," baldly stating that "for centuries and, doubtless, millennia [...], the same beliefs and techniques are reproduced or transmitted, often down to the minutest details." He further added that "witchcraft is sterile and recalcitrant to progress" and its adherents "continue to believe what they have always believed."[1]

French historians, meanwhile, whose goal, one might reasonably suppose, was to explore the historical evolution of witchcraft (and, indeed, all other social forms), have in fact done quite the opposite—and done so, whatever they may claim, with startling epistemological naïveté. Some authors, without a word of justification, simply run together phenomena drawn from quite different epochs and regions, while others (and they are often the same people) draw on the archives of witchfinding institutions as if they were direct ethnographic sources, more or less free from

---

1. Lévi-Strauss 1958. Anglo-American anthropology, for its part, simply denies the existence of this sort of witchcraft in contemporary Europe, a point to which I shall return in chapter 6.

political or ideological bias;[2] others still (and they are legion) find themselves obliged to fall back on ahistorical factors and invoke, for instance, "Magism" or the "animist mentality." Lévi-Strauss' claim that witchcraft as practiced in the province of Berry embodied "permanent modalities of the functioning of the human mind" is no better.

My intention here is to engage in a limited form of historical analysis, by demonstrating that contemporary Bocage witchcraft is the product of a particular form of cultural labor on the part of the local population and that it emerges from an ongoing process of negotiation with the wider, dominant national culture. By comparing some of my data with relevant sources from the nineteenth century, I hope to show that French peasant witchcraft is, in fact, highly varied and adaptable.

COMPARISON OF EXEMPLARY NARRATIVES

What local people call witchcraft is, I have suggested, a form of collective therapy specifically tailored to the family farm and nothing more than that—so-called traditional representations and ritual elements serve to reinforce the therapeutic process. This was something my readings of studies of rural French witchcraft and the works of amateur local folklorists from the nineteenth century had not prepared me for. How to account for this gulf between the analyses of my predecessors and my own? It cannot be explained in terms of differences of method. Of course, unlike the folklorists, I allowed myself to be "caught up" (*prise*) in the chains of bewitchment, variously occupying different positions within the system; and of course, I participated in or observed numerous dewitching treatments, including my own, which gave me access to a wider range of witching discourses, as well as a chance to compare them. In any case, both my predecessors and I did collect examples of one comparable form of oral narrative—the exemplary narrative.

The fact that these have changed radically from one century to another suggests that witchcraft in the Bocage has also changed radically over the same period—a change that must be situated vis-à-vis wider shifts

---

2. Claiming to have spotted a trap does not, it seems, prevent one from falling into it (cf. for example Muchembled 1978 and 1979).

in social techniques the minimization of misfortune (*réduction du mal-heur*). This is a concept I developed in order to process data that might allow for a historical comparison of Bocagite witchcraft. In its current guise, its purpose is to minimize misfortunate events affecting the pro-duction, reproduction, and survival of livestock and people on family farms. I thus examined historical techniques of minimization, both ma-terial (agricultural, mechanical, meteorological, veterinary, medical) and symbolic (witchcraft, "traditional" healing, official and popular religious practices, and psychological therapies), noting what vanished, emerged, or shifted over time.

For reasons of simplicity, I base my comparison here on a single text, Jules Lecœur's *Esquisses du Bocage Normand* (2 volumes, 1883 and 1887),[3] which is both the most encyclopedic of those I have read and is focused on a nearby region. The publication dates suggest that the observations were carried out from perhaps 1850–80, a period of economic bonanza for the French peasantry that *l'Histoire de la France rurale* considers to be the "apogee of peasant civilization" (Agulhon 1976). The second half of the nineteenth century marked the end of periods of scarcity and crises of subsistence, a period when income from stock-rearing and agriculture increased in unprecedented fashion. The old agricultural system, which combined subsistence agriculture and rural crafts, is revolutionized as a market economy for the sale of livestock is set in place and rural crafts go into steady decline (from 1850-1914). From the late-nineteenth century until 1940, grass meadows colonized ever greater areas of useful agricul-tural land. When Lecœur was making his observations, the old cultural system was still in place. Most farmland is arable and harvests are mea-gre; the few meadows are not grazed, but reserved for hay, and are only found in sodden valley bottoms; the only true grazing land is moor, scrub, copse, and heather; and, finally, a little orchard area next to the farmhouse is used to produce cider and perry, as well as for domestic fowl and rabbits (Frémont 1967; Agulhon 1976; Gervais, Jollivet, and Tavernier 1977).

From a religious perspective, the period is marked by the rise, across France as a whole, of new ultramontane religious movements, as the "God of Vengeance" comes to terms with the "God of Love." These practices

---

3. A more complete bibliography of local folklorists can be found in Fournée (1985).

are highly popular with urban women, as well as in rural areas where the faith is still strong, though Gérard Cholvy (1976), the only historian to have examined the question, regrets that he is unable to explain what the peasantry thinks of such practices nor why they adopt them.

This ardent faith contrasts strongly with the abandonment of religion on the part of what Louis Chevalier called the "laboring classes and [the] dangerous classes" (1973) and marks the final passage in a movement away from the stereotype of the pagan peasant (the dim-witted and bestial *paganus*)—a movement that began toward the end of the eighteenth century with the development of "ruralophile" literature. Michel de Certeau, Dominique Julia, and Jacques Revel (1970) remark that the folklorists use of the term "popular" can actually be glossed as "rural." More specifically, it represents a bowdlerized form of rurality expunged of any reference to the peasantry's violence or past political subversion. This literature showcases a primitive peasantry—honest, childlike, naïve, and unaffected, but Christian and respectful of hierarchy.

In Western France, the rural population is almost without exception composed of practicing Christians (unlike in small local towns), and it produces priests, monks, and nuns in significant numbers. The new religious movements are propagated either by specialized priestly societies dedicated to proselytism (devotion of the Way of the Cross) or by parish priests: the Marian devotional movement (with the introduction of the month of Mary and the apparition of the virgin at Our Lady of Pontmain in 1871); the devotion of the Sacred Heart; worship of local saints (only recognized by religious authorities after doing a little symbolic violence to existing theological interpretations); the cult of the dead (All Saints' Day and the introduction of Masses for Souls in Purgatory). Convents are to be found in every small town, where they dispense education and healthcare. Parish life reaches its maximal historical intensity; this period is also the apogee of parish civilization (Cholvy and Hilaire 1985).

Despite its modest title, *Esquisses du Bocage Normand* ("Sketches from the Normandy Bocage") is a veritable regional encyclopaedia covering, in its eight hundred and forty-eight pages, all aspects of local human geography over a hundred-year period and all elements of folklore. Witchcraft takes up sixty pages of this monumental total (Lecœur 1883 and 1887: chapters 1–31).

When it comes to folklore, it is no good making unreasonable demands of Lecœur. For him, the peasant is a repository of discrete cultural traits that he cannot imagine could ever be linked into a logical or symbolic whole. Chapter after chapter and paragraph after paragraph, he transmits what he has gleaned, but we know nothing of where and how he gleaned his harvest: he notably fails to distinguish between what peasants told him and what he drew from traditional oral genres such as tales and proverbs.

As far as witchcraft is concerned, Lecœur only offers the reader exemplary narratives—these tales that "believers" tell to well-disposed audiences, be they known adherents of the faith or simply not obvious skeptics. In all likelihood, Lecœur heard many of these tales himself and he listened without laughing. Of course, he does not himself believe in witchcraft but nor does he avail himself of the opportunity to pour scorn: the capacity and tendency to believe is, he says, universal, and belief in science generates as much superstition as belief in magic.

Lecœur does not, however, even suspect the existence of the second type of narrative we have discussed—the exhortatory tale intended to deal with failures of dewitching and that tell us so much. He never had a chance to hear them. Nor does he consider the importance of mentioning the context in which each tale was told and the relationship between speaker and audience. The failure to do so causes him to group witch and dewitcher under a single term ("*sorcier*"—i.e., witch), though it is always clear from context which is which.

Despite these caveats, the comparison of exemplary narratives from 1887 and 1970 is hugely instructive, illustrating the historical shift in local practices of witchcraft toward a form of therapy directed at the family farm.

We shall compare first the actions and then the agents of witchcraft, before finally turning our attention to local conceptions of "abnormal force."

BEWITCHING AND DEWITCHING

Witchcraft narratives, especially exemplary ones, relate a series of incredible events that defy recognized laws of physical causality. This does not, of course, mean that one can recount just anything: the incredible staging of these events must always be "credible" and this credibility is tightly linked to the prevailing cultural context.

In the nineteenth century, exemplary narratives related a whole series of different bewitching techniques (whether or not they actually existed is beside the point): one does not go the same way about "stirring up" (*monter*) a storm, stopping a moving carriage short, causing a milch cow to dry up (Lecœur gives several methods), making it miscarry or die, or causing a person to languish to death. In contrast, the narratives from 1970, which dwell at such length on the dewitching ritual, have nothing to say about bewitching techniques, simply saying, "the spell was cast" or even "So-and-so did it."

For questions of method, one nowadays has to turn to exhortatory narratives. Their narrators claim that there are several bewitching techniques, but they are incapable of describing them: they roundly insist that bewitching (i.e., the transfer of "force" from one family holding to another) exists but they cannot say how it works. When I asked for further details, my informants speculated that the witch must have used ordinary channels of human communication (speech, gaze, and touch) or they focus on one extremely suspicious element, but failed to locate it in a wider ritual sequence.

For example, in the nineteenth century, narrators might describe the so-called "butter yarn," a technique used for causing a milch cow to dry up. The witch, Lecœur explains, plucked hairs from the cow whose milk he coveted for his own dairy herd and wove them into a yarn, which he then knotted at various points, "saying the appropriate words and tying the knots tied in a particular fashion." The yarn was next tied to the left hind leg of the witch's own cow, which he next took for an early morning walk along the paths and over the grazing lands of the cow whose milk he wished to siphon off.

In 1970, in contrast, people might mention having caught a witch plucking hairs from a cow or wandering around with a handful of such hairs but nobody ever explicitly mentioned the butter yarn, or went into the detail provided in the nineteenth-century versions. And what little detail there was, was undermined by a series of vague distancing techniques: "It was cow hair, or at least it looked like it . . ."

In the same way, people in 1970 still spoke of witches causing people to languish to death but nobody explained how they did so. In 1887, the witch had to pluck a hair from the sleeping victim and then use a needle to sow it between "leather and flesh" while reciting a "secret spell." As the hair grew into the victim's body, he slowly withered away, until at last the ingrown hair reached the heart and tied it in a thousand knots, such that the victim died in unimaginable pain. This was perhaps a credible tale at a time when the church was flooding the countryside with copies of the lives of the saints that people read to one another around the evening fire. Nowadays, people prefer to say that the witch works using direct contact, using the superficially more rational channels of direct communication. (It is worth noting that the idea that human communication can lead to cycles of calamity or suffering is a widespread idea in psychoanalysis.) In contemporary witchcraft, the only metaphorical contact that remains credible is the dewitching rite. And even then, it has to be handled in specific ways, as demonstrated by the following two exemplary narratives, collected a century apart.

In the 1887 version, a bewitched victim, "caught in a death spiral" (*pris à mort*), needs a dewitcher. This latter locks himself away with the dying man and places a brave young lad at the door to listen out for any noises and let the dewitcher know when he hears them. The dewitcher takes a beef heart, hangs it from a hook in the fireplace, and utters a spell while making what Lecœur calls "bizarre gestures." He then takes a long knitting needle and repeatedly stabs the heart until it is all bloody. He stops from time to time to listen, only to start murmuring spells and stabbing anew. The young lad hears no sounds out of the ordinary and so the dewitcher ups the tempo. At last, the lad gives him a sign. A low moan is heard, then others, then heart-rending cries interspersed with prayers and imprecations. A desperate voice begs for mercy, but the dewitcher forbids the lad to open the locked door. Finally, the dewitcher decides it can be opened and a pallid figure can be seen stretched out on the floor, rattling his death and "sweating all his blood" from a thousand cuts. The epilogue states that the witch died "drained of his blood," while the bewitched victim quickly recovered the "rosy hue of good health."

In a comparable version from 1970, the victim has similar symptoms (he sickens or is caught in a death spiral) and the dewitcher makes use of similar techniques, repeatedly stabbing a boiled beef heart in the presence of the entire family. One key difference is that in the 1887 version, the dewitcher makes the family leave the room, while in the modern version he gathers them together for the ritual. Once the rite is complete, the witch (a man called Tripier) comes running up "crazed with the pain of the needles"; he is hospitalized in the middle of the night and a significant part of his intestine has to be removed.

Just as in the tale from 1887, a metaphorical action is supposed to have immediate real-world effects on the absent witch's body, but the elements of the metaphor are quite different. The relationship between these elements is expressed in vague terms. In the earlier version, the witch's body is literally struck with a thousand cuts and is bleeding heavily, whereas in the later version, the witch is simply "crazed with the pain of the needles." What is shocking in the story is not the direct correlation between metaphor and reality, but the fact that the damage done to the witch reflects his name: Tripier, in French, means "gut-monger," or somebody who sells intestines for consumption (this emphasis on the proper noun is, of course, another idea frequently found in psychoanalysis).

THE AGENTS OF WITCHCRAFT

Those who lack "force"

Nowadays, being bewitched is seen as a state of weakness or irremediable lack from which one has no chance of escape on one's own. An ordinary person is defenseless against the "abnormal force" of a witch. It is a combat he cannot win and so his only hope is to appeal to someone possessed of force. Once more, this idea (of an individual or collective subject who has an irremediable weakness and must appeal to someone else to survive) is common in modern psychotherapy.

In the nineteenth century, ordinary people were much better equipped to defend themselves against "abnormal force." The mere fact of being a Christian afforded them a degree of protection and meant that they could often fight their own battles, even in quite serious cases. Anybody, for instance, could make use of the following:

- Prayers and ritual gestures: Satan could be driven back by reciting the Lord's Prayer, or Ave Maria, or by making the sign of the cross either in the air or over oneself.

- Religious symbols: it only took one good Christian's decision to bury holy relics on Mount Margantin [a local landmark] to put an end to the witches' Sabbath held there at the Midsummer solstice.
- Objects that had been blessed, both defensively and offensively: if a sorcerer "stirred up" a storm, anyone could fire a holy bullet until the darkest cloud and the tumult would cease, bring the witch crashing to the ground; and a holy silver bullet could be used against "wolf-running" witches (*meneurs de loups*) that preyed upon livestock.

In the space of a century, bewitched people lost their faith in the protective powers of religious practices alone, and this for two reasons. First, because with the decline of Catholicism as a guiding influence in French society, its rituals have been stripped of their former efficacy; and second, because the Church, caught up in a wider rationalizing movement, gradually stopped endorsing these practices, dismissing them as superstitious: since the 1920s, the general rule has been to scrap them where possible and, failing that, to undermine them. In short, nineteenth-century Christians were symbolically armed with their faith.

Lecœur also claims that age naturally endowed women with "supernatural force," so old women could "undo" or counteract a bewitchment even if they had no "books." As for men, unlike contemporary victims, they did not consider it a metaphysical absurdity to physically compel a witch to relinquish his grip. Rather than seeing a dewitcher, they could threaten or beat a witch to force him to "undo" the bewitchment. What is more, practitioners of particularly vulnerable trades had their own "secret" techniques that allowed them to carry on their work. So drivers, for example, were under constant threat from malevolent shepherds who knew how to stop a stagecoach in its tracks or prevent it from moving off. Lecœur tells of a driver who always traveled with a little hammer, which he used to strike the shoes of his horses while pronouncing an exorcism: his horses trot off untroubled, while the shepherd's flock is scattered and crazed. Finally, anyone who gathered up a poisonous animal without realizing it was temporarily blessed with clairvoyance, allowing him to counteract the witches' spells.

Generally speaking, ordinary people, unlike a dewitcher, might have been incapable of entirely turning the tables on a witch, but they had the wherewithal to counteract certain forms of bewitchment. The symbolic benefits of being a Christian were available to all and the fact that one could gang up on a witch meant that the possibility of physical coercion was also widely available. Other forms of advantage were perhaps intended to compensate for some objective weakness or vulnerability, such as that of an old woman alone on a country road. In the end, though, it matters little how we interpret these traits; the important thing is that they provided people with the means to confront the threat of witchcraft alone without relying on external help and much less *therapeutic* help.

Dewitchers

According to Lecœur, nineteenth-century dewitchers were either country folk or urbanites "well versed in the supernatural sciences"—owners of "books." The second group was mainly composed of priests and, to a lesser extent, doctors. By the twentieth century, techniques for minimizing misfortune and suffering have advanced sufficiently for medical doctors to limit themselves to the natural sciences and priests to rational theology. As such, both groups now fall into the category of "unbelievers" in local witching discourse. Contemporary dewitchers are invariably country folk and local peasants are well aware that witchcraft is not recognized outside their immediate social milieu.

Witches

In the nineteenth century, witches might be either local farmers or outsiders. Shepherds figured foremost among this latter group and this for two reasons: there was no way to control or survey their movements and they acted up because they were not yet married and so did not have responsibility for a farm or holding. Most of their witching was simply mischievous, designed to generate a laugh at another's expense rather than cause damage to a farm: they might bring a moving coach up short, prevent it from moving off, or magically siphon off cider and wine. In short, they were the harmless face of sorcery, the face of youthful high jinx.[4] Next

---

4.   In rural France, in the nineteenth century, the "youth" must be understood as an institution of sorts—one whose purpose was to organize festivities, as well as public rituals of humiliation for remarried widows or cuckolds.

came passing travelers who were more likely to perform harmful witchcraft: beggars, in particular, might react badly if refused alms, but itinerant tradesman (ratters, molecatchers, diviners, etc.) were also a threat.

Nowadays, the shepherds are no more, and the only place one can observe the harmless face of witchcraft is on the American television series *Bewitched.*[5] Vagabonds and itinerant tradesmen have also vanished. The only outsiders who still visit family farms are professional healers and menders: doctors, vets, mechanics; or administrative personnel such as civil servants or salesmen from agricultural firms. Relations between farmers and these new categories of outsiders obey a different logic: the latter may not have a farm of their own but they are not rootless vagrants. This means that modern witches are only to be found among those fellow farmers with whom one entertains social relations and witchcraft episodes are restricted to a single sociological context: agonistic confrontations between farming families. Agricultural laborers (*commis*) are nowadays extremely rare, but they are ideal targets for witchcraft accusations: they are physically close to their employers and have access to all his property and are also in charge of smallholdings. As far as their employers are concerned, they are neither outsiders nor irresponsible.

ABNORMAL FORCE

Trajectories

In the nineteenth century, "force" flowed more freely than today. Even ordinary people (neither witches nor dewitchers) might cast a spell to defend their rights or uphold justice (whence they derived this force, however, is unclear). Lecœur gives the example of a woman who did so in order to rid the region of a band of brigands. Other tales tell of dewitchers who did not limit their activity to attacks on witches at the behest of

---

5. Fifty-four episodes of the series were screened on French television during my fieldwork. In it, a beautiful witch falls in love with an ordinary mortal and marries him after having promised to renounce her magical powers. These, however, are triggered each time she touches her nose, something that she finds herself doing on a regular basis, either to help with the housework or to counteract the spells cast against her husband by her troublesome mother and aunt.

clients but also attacked ordinary people in defense of the moral order or their reputation. For instance, a dewitcher (a doctor) paralyzed a group of gossips who, forgetting that those possessed of force can overhear from afar, decried him as a witch and mocked him.

In the narratives I heard, in contrast, trajectories of force are strictly regulated: it can only travel from a witch to his victim (an ordinary farmer lacking in force) and from a victim's dewitcher to the witch that laid him low. Dewitchers have no cause to exercise their powers outside of this specific context.[6] As a result, the scope of the dewitcher's action has been reduced, but within these new limits, he is the only possible agent, the only person who can resolve a crisis.

Origins

In the nineteenth century, people said that one needed "evil books," "spell books" baptized by Satan, outlining the recipes of the magic kitchen, in order to acquire "force." All those possessed of force were supposed also to possess at least one such book. This included witches and dewitchers, including country spellcasters, priests, and the occasional doctor.

Nowadays, only witches are supposed to possess these books. People do not explicitly say that dewitchers do not have any books: they must have got their secrets from somewhere, perhaps from books, but certainly not from "evil" books or the same books that witches use. When I asked where dewitchers got their "force" from, people never mentioned "spell books," but dwelled instead at inordinate length on the occasion where his "force" was finally recognized: when he cured his own cancer, exposed a witch, or predicted the precise date of a prisoner's return in 1945. In 1970, the dewitcher's force came from his "strong blood," his personal charisma, and nothing else. What is more, witchcraft is now a secular pursuit: Satan no longer has any part to play in the matter and priests with "evil books" are scarcely ever mentioned. This has had a radical impact on the origin stories of witches. Both then and now, the

---

6. More precisely, "abnormal force" is only expressed within the bounds of a particular farm—i.e., within the limits of the social space described by the name of the head of the family—and only affects its bioeconomic potential and reserves.

protagonist is an innocent person who chances upon an "evil book" and reads it almost by accident, but it is no longer the same type of innocent and the results of the encounter are quite different.

In the 1887 version, the "spell book" is chanced upon by someone close to a priest: either his niece or servant (an irresponsible young girl) or alternatively an altar boy or student (perhaps a shepherd, another young person without responsibilities). He (or she) can barely read and haltingly utters out loud words on the page that he cannot fully understand. In so doing, he invokes Satan without meaning to. At the bottom of the page, there is a warning: "turn the page if you dare," but the reader is consumed by curiosity and goes ahead anyway or, in some version, is so nearly illiterate that he cannot even understand the warning. The devil is conjured up, appearing as a man or a great black goat. He bids the young witch issue him with commands, but the latter just looks on dumbly. So Satan pounces upon him and carts him off into the heavens. In the next sequence, the priest reflects on this mysterious disappearance and works out what must have happened. He undertakes a series of increasingly powerful exorcisms until the imprudent young person is at last recovered, more dead than alive, along with the dangerous spell book. The priest tries to burn the book, but it is impervious to flames until the correct exorcistic rite is performed.

In the version from 1970, the "evil book" is chanced upon by a young man who either inherits it or finds it in the farm he has just purchased. He is then a young head of a family and not a young girl or a footloose youth and he immediately understands what he has in his hands. In exhortatory narratives, some bewitched farmers mention just such an event, declaring that they swiftly burned the book without opening it. This seems to be just as difficult a task as it was in the nineteenth century but also a much more dangerous one—perhaps because these book-burners no longer pronounce an exorcism. As a result, the stove may explode or the fireplace cave in. In exemplary narratives, the young man also understands that it is a spell book of black magic, but consumed by curiosity, he reads it from cover to cover. He pays no heed to the warnings at the bottom of pages, which he fully understands and which have become more complicated over the intervening hundred years, now reading: "Turn the page if you dare or if you can" or "if you want to" or "if you desire" (here, once more, as in psychotherapy, we see the importance of desire). The book transforms the young man into a jealous witch, whose touch, speech, and gaze wreak havoc on his victims and allow him to improve his farm without effort; just like anyone possessed of abnormal force, however, the possession is mutual and he is driven to commit a malicious act every day, whether or not he desires it.

Abilities

Lecœur noted that, in 1887, witches had already stopped attending Sabbaths, transmogrifying into animals (horses, hares, wolves, foxes, black goats) so as to terrify and prey upon nighttime travelers, "running wolves," and strangling their enemies' livestock. That said, the witch of 1887 still possessed numerous abilities that I did not hear discussed in 1970. Contemporary witches can no longer "stir up" storms, unleash winds, hail, rain, thunder, or lightning and so fire—be it within the bounds of a farm or across a whole region. People no longer tell of storm-stirrers or cloud-runners who assume the form of a pair of crows who drive the storm from their vantage point atop the darkest cloud. And perhaps because the shepherds are no more (for it was their speciality), witches are no longer credited with the capacity to siphon cider from an apple tree by planting a knife in it, or wine from a barrel by sticking a knife in an oak tree. They have also lost their former ability to stop a coach in its tracks, to startle livestock at a market and so start a stampede, to plague their enemies with fleas (I only heard tell of one old woman who had witnessed it in her youth), or their farms with rats, insects, or other vermin that reduce the harvest. Finally, witches can no longer induce "St. Vitus danse" (which doctors call hysteria[7]) or madness (which they call psychosis); no more can they cause a bewitched person to live like a beast while retaining his human form, crawling on all fours, howling, and roaming the woods before dying in some bush (this has become a form of schizophrenia).

Nowadays, medical institutions are charged with diagnosing and treating these sorts of complaints, which the bewitched may still, deep down, be inclined to attribute to the action of magic. Dewitchers share

---

7.   When there is no neurological basis for the condition; when there is such a base, it is called Huntington's or Sydenham's Chorea.

a similar interpretation of events but even so they avoid so-called crazy clients like the plague, preferring to leave them to the psychiatrists.

What is more, dewitchers are no longer credited with the ability to defuse storms, raging winds, thunder, or fire, or instead to redirect them away from arable lands. Nor can they stir up storms and unleash wind or rain on areas of wasteland simply to prove the extent of their powers. And finally, they can no longer walk through the rain without getting wet. Any nineteenth-century dewitcher worth his salt was, in principle, endowed with these capacities but the tales focus especially on the role of priests as meteorological exorcists. Many priests were reluctant to undertake such obviously superstitious activity and so the local population sometimes had to force their hand. Others though, willingly shouldered the burden—e.g., one priest known locally as the "storm-reaver" (*fendeur d'orage*), who locked himself away in the church in full ritual regalia and pronounced increasingly "forceful" exorcisms until the danger had passed. Other tales tell of his galloping or running to an isolated chapel on the moors, roaring his exorcisms as the storm or fire nipped at his heels.

Witches can, however, still cause people to sicken in a variety of ways and, in particular, to languish to death (though nowadays it is normally called "getting depressed" or "having a nervous breakdown"); they can also make livestock sicken, dry up cows, cause them to miscarry or calve stillborn young, diminish harvests, or wither trees and plants; they can still stop vehicles in their tracks, prevent them from starting, or drive them into ditches (the vehicles are today more likely to be cars or tractors than horse-drawn carts); they can prevent bread from rising (though this now only affects bakers), milk from giving cream, butter from churning (everyone has experienced this, but only in the old days; butter is now bought in shops); they can hear from afar, especially things said about themselves, become invisible, or provoke hallucinations (though there is always a degree of doubt as to whether it wasn't a hallucination linked to "panic attacks" caused by the least contact with a witch).

Similarly, dewitchers can still heal an illness brought about by magic, cause a witch to sicken and die, hear from afar, become invisible to witches, and provoke hallucinations. . . . Simply put, they can do to witches what witches do to others.

This side-by-side comparison of the changing abilities of witches and dewitchers over the course of a century gives a clear idea of the social changes that have taken place in the countryside as well as the local effects of wider processes of rationalization, such as the shift in techniques for the minimization of misfortune and suffering: storm-stirrers and storm-reavers have given way a rationally purified form of belief and greater meteorological knowledge, while interpretations by medicine now cohabit with interpretations by witchcraft, without the exact relationship between the two ever being made clear.

Over the last century, material techniques for minimizing misfortune (agricultural productivity, economic and weather forecasts, animal reproduction, medical treatments for humans and animals) have developed in remarkable ways. Medical institutions have gained in credibility, while traditional healers have been relegated to the margins. Older techniques of symbolic mitigation or repair (institutional religion and "popular" witchcraft) have not vanished entirely, but the abilities with which they are credited have significantly reduced in scope and grown more specialized. The space left by their retreat has been gradually taken over by psychological forms of therapy.

*

Many of the characteristic traits of nineteenth-century witchcraft in the area have now disappeared: the intimate relationship with religion, the belief that ordinary Christians have a degree of supernatural "force," the range of different magical agents, and the existence of benign or harmless forms of magic. Other aspects of the phenomenon have also changed: the content of exemplary narratives has adapted to modern canons of credibility, the abilities associated with "abnormal force" have grown fewer, and the channels along which it can travel are more strictly regimented.

We should not, however, conclude that contemporary witchcraft is a mere survival, a now meaningless remainder of a once vibrant cultural construct. There are two reasons why this is wrong. First, because this cultural construct (viz. nineteenth-century witchcraft) is now definitively beyond our reach: the exemplary narratives collected by folklorists are insufficient to allow us to reconstruct it. And second, because what these narratives can show us is what witchcraft was *not* at the time they were collected: there is nothing to suggest that it functioned at the time as a sort of collective therapy for members of a family farm.

It was no small thing to create this specific form of therapy, for which there was no existing model in France; on the contrary, it required a vast work of culture. Witchcraft was stripped of those elements that did not contribute to this end and new ideas were introduced—those that I have flagged as also part of the psychotherapeutic tradition doubtless evolved in parallel with this latter. This has completely reconfigured the field of abnormal force. For a cultural construct possessed of a "limited adaptability," this is no small feat.

Chapter Four

"Oh the witch, the filthy bitch, your neighbor . . ."

In talking cures, the therapist's task primarily consists in gradually and imperceptibly enveloping the patient's complaint in a mental formation that is neither entirely imaginary nor entirely realist; it is enough that it be plausible. In this way, the therapist opens up a semifictional space of "play" where the ailment can progressively be stripped of its hyperreality and stability. The particular expression taken by the complaint, the therapist's gender, the nature of the mental construct in operation, the manner in which it is expressed, and the flexibility it affords the participants—all these things are culturally encoded and it is the task of the anthropologist to describe and compare them.

Dewitching as I experienced it in the Bocage can be understood in these terms. Officially, the only thing it involves is a dewitching ritual, but as I have mentioned, the ritual itself actually only plays a modest part in the overall process. The dewitcher in fact undertakes a whole series of other actions to help resolve the crisis and enjoins the patients to do as much. Together, these actions constitute a form of family therapy adapted to a farming unit, involving a psychological shift that takes several months. By exploring the work of Madame Flora, a clairvoyant dewitcher whom I witnessed at work (both on myself and others) over a period of two years, we can see how this therapy is carried out using an adapted form of cartomancy that she developed herself.

THE THERAPEUTIC FRAME

From a practical point of view, a dewitching cure with Madame Flora takes the following form: the first three séances take place at nine-day intervals, then they occur on a monthly basis for a minimum of four sessions. The séance lasts roughly two hours and takes place in Madame Flora's small dining room. The bewitched couple normally attends together, often with their children. In 1970–72, a séance cost roughly 40 francs[1]: ten francs for the card-reading and thirty francs to pay for the votive candles and masses that Madame Flora claimed to offer for the victims in a miraculous chapel of the Virgin.

After a perfunctory exchange of civilities, Madame Flora begins to draw the cards—this takes about an hour and a quarter with a 32-card piquet deck (i.e., standard cards) and three-quarters of an hour with a nineteenth-century Lenormand tarot deck.[2] She then recommends to them a series of rituals to be performed at home, giving them to understand that once she is alone, she will "do the necessary" (a local euphemism for dewitching).

The most immediately striking aspect of the sessions is how energetic they are. The clients arrive for the first séance confused, downcast, and apathetic and by the end have generally perked up a good deal. Though Madame Flora is liable to see no end of catastrophes in the cards (including the precise and very short time they have left to live if they leave things untreated), the patients act as if a weight had been removed from their shoulders. "At last we know where we stand," they exclaim as they leave the room. By the end of the third session, they are rejuvenated. They look forward to the séance, engage passionately with the process, and leave with the impression that their life resembles a film or a novel. The question is how the dewitcher injects them with such vigor using only a deck of cards and her silver tongue.

---

1. Some forty euros (US$60) in today's money.
2. *Grand Jeu de société et de pratiques secrètes de Mlle Lenormand* [54 cards with explanatory book]. Published in 1845 in Paris by B. P. Grimaud.

HEALING THE UNWITTING

The bewitched portray themselves as hapless innocents struck down by repeated and baffling misfortune. Their health is ailing, their livestock dying, their fields infertile, and their children cowed. They, meanwhile, are honest, industrious, helpful Christians whose solitary aim is to maximize the good. How could anyone wish them harm? How could anyone wish the deaths of such good people ("we were raised to turn the other cheek")? They repeatedly stress that their only experience of evil has been to have it inflicted upon them and all they ask of the dewitcher is to protect them from it.

As the principal symptom of bewitchment is a lack of force, Madame Flora's goal is to restore it. And like all dewitchers, she knows where the missing force can be found: with those who have too much, and in those practices and dispositions that characterize the witch—hatred, violence, and aggression. She cannot, however, announce this so bluntly to the bewitched family that wants only what's good. She cannot say, "If it's force you need, then you must be like witches: mean, low, jealous." They would spit on her. So instead, she must help them connect with a capacity for violence and evil without their ever realizing it; she must help them embrace the dark side without ever making it explicit and without forcing them to recognize this.

This deception relies on Madame Flora's ability to behave as if she herself played no direct role in the card-reading, merely passing on the message. At the start of the first séance, the dewitcher knows nothing about the specifics of the family's situation. She then immediately begins to shuffle the deck, beginning anew each time a card falls out of the pack or flips over; all to show that the order of the cards is out of her hands. The head of the family is called upon to cut with his left hand and spread twelve cards out facedown in a semicircle and then to cover them each with six more cards, dealt in the same way. In this way, responsibility for the messages to come is firmly transferred to him—he is directly responsible, for it is he who cuts and deals the cards and, at the same time, he is innocent because he uses the hand he least controls.

Madame Flora then counts the cards off ("1, 2, 3, 4, 5") and flips over the fifth card: "this is you" (the head of the family; then "1, 2, 3, 4, 5: and this is your wife." "1, 2, 3, 4, 5: the deck is telling us to wait"; "1, 2, 3, 4, 5: let's see what the jack of spades is telling us.") In short, it is "the deck" and the "jack of spades" who transmit the messages to the assembled company (including the dewitcher), who collectively called for them and collectively wait to see what will be revealed. "1, 2, 3, 4, 5. . ." and Madame Flora only interprets the card if she already has an idea of what to say; otherwise, she passes over it and counts again: "1, 2, 3, 4, 5." Little by little, each of the cards she reveals acquires an entourage that alters its meaning in different ways, depending on whether it is to the right, the left, or on another layer. This allows her either to correct a hasty assertion or elaborate a more complex statement. It is worth thinking about this as a form of language. Each card is a word and a suite of cards, a sentence.

As she works her way through the decks, Madame Flora becomes increasingly assertive. For instance, after half an hour, the husband may rebel against the third appearance of a particular "sentence." But Madame Flora knocks him back with a peremptory "Just look at the cards you dealt here [e.g., a nine of spades, symbolizing death]! And there! And there!" If he still contests the reading, she takes a tarot interpretation book from a little briefcase and shows them a picture of the card, which features not only the standard suit markings but also a multicolored image with a little inscription below ("Death," "Landowner," "Lawman," "Wicked woman") and a judgment on the nature of a person or situation ("Arguments and anguish," "False flatterer," "Chatterbox").[3] Madame Flora highlights the particular verbal or visual element that supports her interpretation and presents it to the client as an absolute proof. The bewitched family sits in front of the card table and listens to Madame Flora's running commentary on the cards, rather as they would listen to a radio broadcaster comment on a football match. In both cases, they try to represent what they see and hear to a listener who has no direct access to the spectacle.

The cards are, by definition, capable of representing every element of the clients' lived world: people, animals, plants, machines; but also thoughts and acts; past, present, and future events; real, potential, and even imaginary events. And as they sit and listen, they see Madame Flora draw connections between aspects of their lives that they are ordinarily quite careful to keep separate. Quite ordinary cards dealing with the nitty-gritty of daily life are followed by cards that concern the realm of the imaginary (in the broadest possible sense). A single card separates self and other, one's thoughts and acts, one's own thoughts and those

---

3. *Art de tirer les cartes avec le Petit Cartomancien ou Petit Lenormand*. Paris: Grimaud.

Nine of Spades. The caption ("Death"), the ultraconventional image of a skeleton with a scythe, and the associated judgment[4] (losses of all kind, including loss of life) are pleonastic. In any case, fortune-tellers' clients always know what a nine of spades stands for. But even a card whose meaning is so fixed still allows for a good deal of interpretative freedom, which Madame Flora makes the most of: death, of course, is in the cards, but whose death? The witch's? The bewitched client's if he is slow to defend himself? Someone already dead? Somebody yet to die? Quite possibly, if the client fails to follow the protective recommendations? Et cetera.

Ten of Spades. The captions states "Sorrow and tears," but Madame Flora never reads the card without adding "Look: HYPOCRISY, sorrow, and tears." This stress on an unwritten word ("hypocrisy") sheds light on those printed ("sorrow and tears") and reaches beyond the image itself: the weeping peasant woman standing next to the corpse of her dog is seen as a victim of hypocrisy—doubtless that of her "neighbor" (the false friend) who poisoned the animal. The mere concatenation of these different notions, "hypocrisy" (a phonemic suite), death of a chattel (interpretation of one element of the image), and social proximity (obvious but unvoiced), calls for a diagnosis of witchcraft. The card neither states nor shows this, but the fortune-teller's voice is the missing element in the equation, tying everything into the world of witchcraft. Finally, she blithely ignores the possibility that the judgment might be, in Miss Lenormand's words, "upended"[5] ("short-term punishment") as it goes against the whole idea of witchcraft: it may well be written on the card in black and white, but for Madame Flora, it does not count.

---

4. Miss Lenormand calls it a "prognosis."
5. The accompanying booklet does not specify in which conditions a judgment may be "upended." The term doubtless refers to combinations of cards (two aces or three kings) or the context in which a card is drawn (e.g., a ten of spades next to a queen of diamonds).

of another, thoughts one has had and might have had, the accident avoided last week (but which Madame Flora recounts in minute detail), and yesterday's difficult calving. It is, of course, the dewitcher who draws the links between a given card and a particular element of the bewitched's lived world. She decides that the ace of spades followed by the nine of hearts refers to the imminent death wished upon him or her but which is avoided by magical prophylaxis. In another context, Madame Flora might have decided that this combination of cards referred to a neighbor's jealousy of one's bountiful harvest of beets.

Over the course of the séance, the dewitcher continues to interpret the cards, assigning them a judgment of attribution and fleshing them out by fitting them into episodes she presents in the form of an extended commentary (e.g., of the accident one might have had last week, had the witch had his way) or a real-time commentary of, say, the witch's behavior at the moment the cards are being turned. However, this constant process of interpretation is masked by the claim that the messages and performance are provided by the cards themselves and that they are quite independent of human will, especially that of Madame Flora.

VIOLENCE SHIFTERS

A standard card set is based around the basic contrast between red and black suits (diamonds and hearts vs. clubs and spades). Madame Flora plays on this opposition to develop a rhetorical interpretive strategy based on the idea of antithesis. So, she subtly shifts from the antithesis of colors (red vs. black) to one of properties (dark vs. light cards) and thence to the metaphorical elaboration of these properties:

Red = light = good
Black = dark = evil.

Obviously, the clients can clearly see that there are red and black cards on the baize, but they pay little attention to Madame Flora's endowing them with ethical and ontological significance.

Red = light = good = bewitched
Black = dark = evil = witch.

Queen of Diamonds. The caption ("Evil woman"), the image (a common woman who, in a fit of rage, smashes a chair), and the two printed judgments ("Evil woman, gossip, slanderer" and "She will do you a disservice or cause you harm") all concur: the witch, the "sly old bitch," is her.

Queen of Spades. The caption ("Widow") reflects Madame Flora's prediction almost perfectly ("In time, you will be widowed"), as does the image of a grieving woman[6] seated on a chair and turned away from her mirror and one of the two printed judgments: "Widow or woman living alone with her grief." As for the other judgment, which is supposed to hold if the "prognosis" is "upended" ("Wishes to remarry. Problems"), Madame Flora simply ignores it.

---

6. Madame Flora, of course, makes no mention of the fact that the widow in the image is a stylish urbanite.

And the reason they pay no attention to this shift is that the distribution of values around the antithesis of colors perfectly corresponds to the way they see themselves and the witch. To be bewitched is to be utterly good, and so utterly distant from the witch, who is perfectly evil.

Careful observation of Madame Flora's spiel revealed, however, her use of a formal technique for establishing a bridge between the patients and the forces of evil and violence associated with the witch. I call this technique the "violence shifter."

Madame Flora introduces two highly significant exceptions to the division of cards into:

Red = light = good = bewitched
Black = dark = evil = witch.

These two exceptions concern the female figures active in a witchcraft episode, who are represented by cards of the "wrong" color:

1) A (female) witch is always represented by the queen of diamonds—i.e., a red, light, and supposedly good card;
2) The bewitched woman (if she attends a consultation alone because her husband is held up) is represented by the queen of spades—i.e., a black, dark card implying evil. When the queen of spades makes an appearance in such a context, Madame Flora invariably says, "In time, you will be widowed." If the husband is present, then the wife is not represented by any particular card; this fits with prevailing agricultural ideology, which assimilates all members of the family to the man whose name is used to designate the farm. The queen of spades is then treated like any other spade.

The male figures implicated in a witching episode are, in contrast, symbolized by cards of the appropriate color:

1) A male witch is the king of spades—so, black, dark, and evil;
2) The bewitched man is the king of diamonds—so red, light, and good. The appearance of the king of diamonds is accompanied by the comment, "You come to bring justice"—i.e., you will, in the near future, bring your enemy to justice.

Thus, the deck's two central couples (the king and queen of spades and diamonds), whose role is to represent the protagonists of a witching crisis, are switched. The two members of the bewitched couple are visually and symbolically paired with the two members of the bewitching couple:

- the king of diamonds (the bewitched man) with the queen of diamonds (female witch)
- the queen of spades (bewitched woman) with the king of spades (male witch).

Patients do not appear to pick up on this switch, nor was it something I noticed while in the field. Even the implicit recognition of these pairings serves, however, to build a bridge between the bewitched couple and the forces of violence and malevolence. And Madame Flora's patter makes almost no perceptible reference to this shifter . . . whence its redoubtable efficacy.

For the dewitcher never pretends that the queen of diamonds (i.e., the witch) is a good card because it is red and light. She neither suggests, nor even hints, that the witch might be good. To the contrary, she unleashes the full force of her rhetorical venom against the "sly old bitch" (*rempâtée salope*). At the same time, though, she forces the bewitched man implicitly to recognize that he is symbolically linked to the witch by virtue of his association with the king of diamonds.

No more does Madame Flora claim that the queen of spades (i.e., the bewitched wife who attends a séance alone) is a good card, as it is black and is a harbinger of death: "In time you will be widowed." The dewitcher also avoids suggesting that the bewitched woman (who is, by definition, good) is symbolized by an evil card. Here again, she simply compels the client implicitly to recognize that she is paired with the king of spades (the witch) by virtue of her association with the queen of spades. And she also cleverly encourages her to make the most of the advantages this identity confers upon her: "You! You are strong," she declares. Not like your feeble husband and that is why you will be widowed—you will outlive him. Each time the wife arrives alone, this presumption of violence is ratcheted up a notch, for armed with the conviction that she at least is strong, the wife exhorts and cajoles her husband behind the scenes, making use of the ordinary tools of marital manipulation.

This technique (the violence shifter) is both necessary and insufficient. It is, of course, quite clear that simply declaring "The queen of diamonds is the witch" is not enough to produce an effect on the person represented by the king of diamonds (the patient). The same is true of his wife: merely saying "You! You are strong" will not suddenly make her embrace violence. Madame Flora makes use of a whole battery of rhetorical techniques to hammer the message home. What follows are a few examples of this.

The dewitcher may flip over a card and instead of commenting on it, give a little cry of horror: "Aaah!" Then her face grows somber and she turns over three more black cards without saying a word. With the fifth she murmurs, "I thought so" between her teeth. If the sixth or seventh card then happens to be a queen of spades, she abruptly slams it down. She then grabs hold of her cane, hammers it against the table, and blurts out, in crescendo, "Oh the witch, the filthy bitch, your neighbor, the queen of diamonds: she wants you dead!" (a set phrase used to indicate the witch). Madame Flora then gathers up the preceding cards and lays them down one by one: "There you go. She brings a plague upon your house"; "But oh how subtle it is"; "Maybe she didn't bewitch you, but she got somebody to do it"; "She's the bitch who's eyeballing your back." She also deploys effects of style to draw the clients along with her: the use of internal rhyme (witch, bitch) and alliteration (bitch, eyeballing, back, but, bring, bewitch), which reinforces the idea of the slow, perfidious, insidious labor of witchcraft: the climbing crescendo of evil.

THE DECK OF CARDS AS THERAPEUTIC JOURNEY

French cartomancy manuals place great emphasis on the choice of standard playing cards or tarot cards, as well as on different reading techniques. They also speak of the standard symbolism of cards as if they predetermined the petitioner's fate. In fact, by choosing a particular deck, deal, or interpretive technique, the reader simply arms herself with a minimal cognitive apparatus that covers the basic vectors of human desire and preoccupation. The art of reading involves successively and incrementally constructing acceptable statements regarding the client's personal situation. This requires a constant exchange of information (verbal or otherwise) between the two partners—the key point, of course, is that the client neither notices nor remembers this exchange. Of course, this central aspect of the reader's art is entirely absent from the manuals.

Madame Flora's customized set of seventy-four cards is made up of two separate decks (one red-backed and one blue-backed). Each deck contains the cards from six to king in each suit, plus the two jokers. Going through my recordings of the sessions, it is clear that Madame Flora respects (without cheating) the rules of interpretation that she devised and though she accords herself a degree of liberty, it is limited.

We can say, for the sake of simplicity, that thirty-four of the cards have fixed meanings and forty have free-floating meanings.

Cards with fixed meanings

These include twenty-four cards that serve as the skeleton of Madame Flora's rhetorical edifice: twenty cards that evoke a turn for the worse (her subject of predilection) and four that evoke a turn for the better—i.e., the triumph of the bewitched family, which takes the form of harm done to the witches. Each of the cards is endowed with a particular meaning: "illness" and "death" are quite distinct, as are "hypocrisy, tears, afflictions" and "divorce." These "malevolent" cards sit well with Madame Flora's taste for hyperbole and she reserves her finest lyrical flights for them.

The other ten fixed cards have a vague positive signification. Madame Flora uses them to slake her clients' thirst for the good and dull their resistance to potential aggression. She can patter away indefinitely about these "favorable" cards, using one-size-fits-all expressions and generally imprecise terms, apparently saving her strength for more important moments: "The omen is good," "Great triumphs ahead," "Really couldn't be better."

The thirty-four cards with a fixed meaning embody a discourse on good and evil—the discourse of witchcraft itself. The twenty-four cards associated with evil correspond to the view of the dewitcher or of the bewitched once they have grown combative and determined to trade blows with the witch, while the ten remaining cards correspond to the perspective of the clients when they first arrive and are still wedded to the good. The little they have to say (what's good is good) can be summed up in a single phrase, even though it is spread over ten cards.

Over the course of the reading, these thirty-four cards are the only ones that Madame Flora refers to by name: "ten of spades, hypocrisy, tears, affliction," "Oh the witch, the filthy bitch, your neighbor . . . the queen of diamonds." The appearance of one of these cards requires a commentary, though it may be held in abeyance for the purposes of building dramatic suspense (as we have already seen). She never ignores one of these cards, however. Nor can just any old remark be made regarding these cards. Madame Flora would never turn over a queen of diamonds and say "Oh, what a lovely neighbor you've got there." Indeed, Madame Flora's credibility depends in part on the clients' ability to quickly recognize these key cards (which appear several times in a session) and thus to see that her interpretations are not arbitrary.

Cards with free-floating meanings

The remaining forty cards have no fixed meaning. When these cards appear, they may not be remarked on and, when they are, the statements are either inconsistent (vaguely positive or negative and conveying limited information) or arbitrary (there is nothing to indicate why a particular card elicits a particular comment).

When Madame Flora turns these cards over, she neither gives an impression of boredom (as with the ten favorable cards) nor of excitement, as when she is lucky enough to flip a "malevolent" card. How then does she respond to them? She uses them to delve into the clients' various concerns and preoccupations regarding the different aspects of their daily lives. These range from an unavoidable encounter with the witch to a delicate interaction with the authorities or dealings with someone whose intentions are opaque. Madame Flora refers to these preoccupations as "thoughts" and she encourages clients to "ask the cards" for more information about any issues they may have.

When she draws one of the cards with a fixed meaning and uses it to elaborate the discourse of witchcraft, Madame Flora only offers up affirmative or exclamatory sentences. When, in contrast, she uses the forty remaining cards to delve into the "thoughts" of her clients, her tone is interrogative: "Perhaps there's some problem with the swine at the moment. . . . Is that it?" As she puts forward these hypotheses and follow-up questions, her voice grows ethereal and weightless and she speeds up so much that the clients scarcely have time to hear their own answers. "You don't say anything; she just guesses right," they marvel afterward. "She just reads you like a book."

One might say that the reading acts out a therapeutic journey. The reader uses the free-floating cards to convert the formless mass of unprocessed emotion, anxiety-inducing situations, and traumatic episodes that paralyze the clients during the early stages of the cure into "thoughts"— easily remembered formulas. Madame Flora engages in a new process of negotiation for each separate "thought"—a negotiation that only comes to an end when the clients meekly allow it to be reformulated in the terms provided by the discourse of evil. Where necessary, she is patient enough to let particular "thoughts" continue to gravitate around the ten "favorable" cards for several readings.

The meanings of the cards describe, then, the discursive formations that the "thoughts" must pass through on the journey toward dewitching. Each time Madame Flora expresses some aspect of the clients' lived world in the form of a "thought," she effects a minimal symbolic operation; each time she transfers a "thought" formulated in the terms of the discourse of ordinary life into the discourse of evil, she offers her clients a therapeutic proposition; and each time they are able to take up this proposition and make it their own, they dewitch themselves.

PROOF BY TAROT[7]

While reading the ordinary cards, the dewitcher repeatedly explores questions of the patients' current situation and their shifting relationships with the witch, going over the information several times. The switch to tarot cards, then, is not designed to elicit further information but to imprint on the patients' minds what has already been revealed by the ordinary cards through the strategic use of visual and aural stimuli (the images on the tarot cards and Madame Flora's rhythmic, metaphorical patter). As with the ordinary cards, the reading addresses various aspects of farm life, this time doing so in a more poetic, refined register.

The fifty-four-card Lenormand Tarot set is, from a graphic point of view, extremely complex. Each card contains the following elements (drawn in a wide array of colors): a miniaturized normal card-face, an

---

7. Reproductions of the relevant cards can be found on pages 64–80.

astrological sign, a floral emblem, and, finally, three scenes or "subjects" (one large and the others small).

The dewitcher focuses all her attention on certain of these "subjects," ignoring the remaining clutter. The deck contains 156 different scenes, of which Madame Flora only commented on roughly a third: those depicting death, devouring, poisoning, imprisonment, abduction, war (conducted by mythological heroes), or marvel—in short, those cards that feed into her penchant for hatred, violence, "force," and the witch's death. Of course, her interpretation of the cards bears strictly no relation to the interpretation proposed by the deck's supposed inventor and Madame Flora blithely reduces Greek mythology to its figurative elements, which she interprets literally (e.g., as an act of violence or a marvel).

The dewitcher elaborates on these images, making inspired pronouncements that the clients are rarely able to resist. Even the most resistant to the call of evil wilt in the face of a particularly elegant rhetorical flight and begin to wish death and torture upon their witch. They are defenseless in the face of the successive waves of visual and aural evidence of the threats that hover over them: the threat of being battered down, like the walls of Troy, by this "fierce steed who sweeps all in his path"; or shot like this hero stood before the firing squad. These images flash at the speed of adverts in front of the clients' eyes, as Madame Flora's voice fleshes them out, twists their meaning, and adds further palimpsestic layers of meaning (the interpretations do not need to be coherent to be effective). The combination of flash cards and metaphors provokes a melee of archaic images in the clients. And at the same time, a stranger who has sloughed all civility and all sense of measure begins to preach vengeance without quarter and terrible death.

As might be expected, the memory often erases this part of the session, as it draws the clients too far down the path of violence, forcing them to embrace, quite unwittingly, the dark side.

NEUTRALIZING THE ANXIETY-INDUCING FIELD

The bewitched, by definition, are lacking in force. Part of their condition is the incapacity to stand toe-to-toe either with the witch or with their business partners or representatives of the bureaucratic order. When the dewitcher notices that the client feels intimidated or threatened by one of these figures and so risks losing the struggle without putting up a fight, then she intervenes first as herself and then as intermediary for the cards. She begins to ask constant questions and tell the client how he should behave (aggressively) in unending detail. She runs through the possibilities one by one: "If they ask you to pay up, you say that, you know, you're happy to pay but you want them to show you the papers!" She plays the part of both sides of the story, offering a solution to every possible situation. She thus maps out the field of the possible with such precision that the client, when he eventually comes face-to-face with his opponent, will have a detailed guide for how to behave. Even if events take a turn that the dewitcher failed to see, the defensive-aggressive behavioral schemas she provided the client with allow him to come up with a suitable response. He is helped in this by the thought that he will be able to recount the episode to Madame Flora the next time he comes and she will doubtless applaud his behavior.

As she runs over these detailed explanations of concrete situations, Madame Flora repeatedly stresses the importance of maintaining a firm distinction between the client qua person and the great abstract principles of Law and Truth that she exhorts him to embody. For instance, she might say, "You're not asking on your own behalf, you're asking because it's your right," or "You're not saying anything wrong; what you say is the truth." When she discusses an interview with the bank manager or a buyer for a lot of pigs, she reminds the client that there is something more fundamental at stake: the ethical order of the world. It is this ethical order that he is charged with defending, for if he manages to convince himself that it is not really him, qua person, who is caught up in this stressful event, then he will be able to meet his opponent with calm force.

PRESCRIBING ACTIONS

At the end of the first session, Madame Flora outlines a program of action that the clients must immediately put into action. First, she provides them with a wealth of detail about how to procure the sometimes distant ingredients necessary to make her apotropaic prescriptions: a little red canvas sachet containing blessed salts, a piece of a paschal candle, and a medal of Saint Benedict; charcoal soaked in a soup plate full of holy water; a little plank all stuck through with nails, et cetera. The bewitched have to learn the protective prayers she dictates to them, in which she leaves the name of the witch or witches blank so the clients are forced to fill them in themselves. In other words, the responsibility for naming the enemy falls on the shoulders of the bewitched and naming, in witching thought, is an act of supernatural aggression that sets in motion a fatal sequence. These prayers must be recited morning, midday, and night, as well as any time they meet a suspected witch (however harmless the situation may seem) or have suspicions about somebody new. Finally, just like all dewitchers, she outlines the long list of magical protections they must put in place (see chapter 2). The most important of these are told in the form of exemplary narratives to make them unforgettable. Over the course of subsequent séances, she will come back to them under a range of pretexts: either because some fresh misfortune has struck (in which case, she narrates an additional layer of protection) or because the bewitched family are unsure about somebody they had not seen for a long time or a stranger seen wandering about the farm. Thus new layers of protection are added to the old ones, while some older ones are quietly abandoned, and new tales are added to the stock of exemplary tales. Little by little, the clients' lives come to be buttressed by this set of acts and behavioral schemas and they begin to report back to the dewitcher with examples of rediscovered initiative.

THE THERAPIST'S VOICE AS ACT OF ENFOLDING

The therapeutic apparatus developed by Madame Flora thus comprises three distinct elements, given a semblance of continuity by the reading of the cards. Were one to ask the clients what Madame Flora does in a séance, they would all (including me, who attended roughly two hundred séances) reply that "she reads the cards and that's it." It was only when Josée Contreras and I sat down and examined the transcripts of my recordings that we noticed the other elements (neutralization of the anxiety-inducing field and the prescribing of actions). We then swiftly realized that the card-reading itself only takes up about half of the time, but that clients fail to recognize that as the process of neutralization is enfolded in the reading of the cards and the prescriptions intermingle with various trivialities at the end of the session.

What really knits the séance together is Madame Flora's voice, which seizes hold of the client as soon as he enters the room and never lets him go, not even for a single second. It covers all possible registers (drama, intimacy, tenderness, ferocity) but above all, it switches from one to the other with preternatural dexterity and never leaves the client to his own devices. This generalized enfolding of the patient in the therapist's voice is an essential element of the "treatment" she offers her clients. It now remains for us to develop an analysis that draws on both musicology and clinical psychology.

The Witch

Madame Flora is quite ignorant of classical mythology and history (one of Miss Lenormand's central themes). She focuses instead on the idea that this hybridity of man and animal represents the witch's dual nature: "a human head with four legs like an animal."

The Witch

For Madame Flora, this Cynocephalus (chosen by Miss Lenormand to illustrate an innocent three of hearts: "a spirit") is a hybrid and so a witch.

The Witch

Miss Lenormand interprets the scene as representing "the god Pan" who chang-es into a "Capricorn" to escape the Giant who is climbing up into the heavens after him. Madame Flora simply turns the inventor's moral assumption on its head: the witch is just such a hybrid creature, one who here flies without wings, borne by a cloud: "a flying goat with legs."

The Predatory Witch and his Prey: 1

The Lenormand deck contains more than a hundred images of animals, often of predator and prey, which Madame Flora interprets as witch and bewitched. It is no problem that the bewitched person is represented by a toad (an unpleasant animal); the toad is little, while the eagle is huge.

The Predatory Witch and his Prey: 2

Early on in the dewitching process, Madame Flora explains the importance of the "predator-prey: witch-bewitched" parallel. From then on, as soon as one of these cards appears, the client's gaze is drawn to the prey, to the exclusion of all else. Here, Madame Flora again inverts Miss Lenormand's interpretation, wherein the good character is the sleeping crocodile and the evil one is the ich-neumon who "slips into its mouth to eat away at its heart."

The bewitched person may be capable of slaying a mythical seven-headed ser-
pent, but he is about to be killed by a mere "scorpion": "look how cunning it
is!" (Miss Lenormand sees a crayfish sent by Juno to Heracles during his battle
against the Hydra.)

Madame Flora sees the witch balancing on a chariot, despite the furious gallop of the "raging horses" (for Miss Lenormand, it shows Achilles dragging Hector's lifeless body around the walls of Troy). The clairvoyant further notes that the card is an eight of spades and death is also to be found in the two minor subjects.

"Somebody wants to cut your life thread."

"Look how you are robbed and consumed."

The witch is a "fierce steed who sweeps all in his path"; the bewitched person is symbolized by the broken-down door, the stormed city and the powerless soldiers.

The queen of diamonds is, of course, the witch, depicted as a furious woman with tousled hair in the main scene (discord at the feast of Thetis and Peleus), and in the minor scene to the bottom left, the bewitched, represented as a nest of eggs being swallowed by a snake.

Madame Flora: "Look at these devils who poison your meals" (Miss Lenormand sees harpies defiling the food of Blind Phineus, King of Thrace).

"Just look at the wild beast [the witch] in your bedroom." For Miss Lenormand, this narcissistic panther represents the "prodigal and dissolute woman."

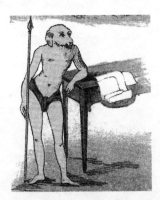

Another witch as human-animal hybrid.

Classical witch behavior: thieving, dreaming up some misdeed, or plotting with somebody else.

Queen of Spades: "In time, you will be widowed."

The inventive Miss Lenormand could not but alight upon the card's obvious symbolism: "Isis, in tears, looking for the husband she finds dead . . ."

"Your face is stung."

"You are being taken for a child and led wherever the witch wants."

"You are being hotted up."[8]

"There you are, in front of the firing squad."

"In time you will be widowed," *suite sans fin*.

---

8. Madame Flora also expresses the same message using ten tarot cards representing an artist or a hermeticist tending to the flame of a philosopher's lamp.

CHAPTER FIVE

Those left behind by the symbolic order

Just as with familiar psychological therapies, dewitching requires a long-term and committed relationship between therapist and client. The creation of such a relationship is made possible by the two parties' shared faith in dewitching. Its longevity depends on the dewitcher's capacity to keep the clients on tenterhooks, shifting back and forth between the quotidian banality of their lives and its simultaneous translation into the epic register of witchcraft. The dewitcher aims to help them recover their lost "force" and learn how to wield indirect violence, by dint of recommendations of apotropaic actions and aggressive noncommunication. I would simply refer to this as "aggression," were it not that I am anxious to avoid reducing dewitching to just another technique of self-assertiveness; as we shall anon, a certain legal but very real violence is necessary to produce a happy farmer.

Dewitching cannot, then, be reduced to a simple behavioral therapy, though the bewitched do indeed learn useful behavioral techniques. Nor is it simply a form of family therapy, as dewitching focuses exclusively on extrafamilial communication—between the bewitched families and bewitching, the latter of which serves as a surface on which to depict a part-real, part-fictive narrative with multiple twists and turns. The bewitched family, meanwhile, is treated as a united group and this unity cannot be called into question: they collectively suffer from the lack of "force" and no family member can be accused of bewitching any other. They stand or fall together.

The reader will recall, however, that Madame Flora interpreted the cards differently depending on whether it was the couple or just the wife who came to consult with her; the use of the violence shifter, which symbolically links the two members of the bewitched couple to their partners in the bewitching couple, is only deployed if the wife comes alone. Should we then think of this technique as mere psychological manipulation, as, say, a plot between women to denigrate men? If, on the other hand, the technique is as central as I have suggested (by giving it such a solemn name) how can Madame Flora be sure that the wife will come alone at some point? Well, quite simply, my experience suggests that she always will and that this always happens in the third session. On that day, particular structural aspects of the bewitched couple are revealed[1] and it is these that we explore in this chapter.

STATE SANCTIFICATION OF CUSTOM

The much-lauded solidarity of the bewitched family unit may be extremely impressive when seen from the outside, but it does not prevent the existence of deep inequalities of status between different members of the family. For locals, a farmer's possessions (both inanimate and animate) have no ontological independence: they have no meaning of their own and are, literally, of one body with him—more precisely, they help make up his body. What is more, French agricultural law and regulations of the 1960s did not contradict these ideas; far from it: by requiring that agricultural enterprises have a single manager, they presented the man (head of family and head of farm) as sole master of the capital and family labor, setting him apart from the family help—i.e., his wives and children of both sexes (even when adult, so long as they still lived on the farm).[2]

---

1. During my fieldwork, I not only attended Madame Flora's séances but I also often drove to the session and back with them—trips of at least two hours. I also visited them at their houses, where we discussed things informally.

2. Locals understand the entire person (body included) to be at the disposal of the head of the family farm, while in national-level legal conceptions of family farms, he only disposes of their capital and labor.

An unmarried man or woman can, of course, set up on their own, so long as they have the means and acquire the status of head of a farm. But unless they have a family (i.e., a source of unpaid labor), such holdings are generally extremely precarious. Marriage, though, introduces a fundamental difference of status between men and women in the world of farming. The male head of a farm who marries keeps his means of production and status. A woman in the same position loses her status when she marries or forfeits her right to it: her husband becomes head of the farm, even if he brings no means of agricultural production to the union, even if he comes from another profession and now intends to set himself up as a farmer. In all these cases, the wife becomes family help and so occupies a subaltern position (just like children of both sexes who live and work on the farm) and she will remain so as long as the marriage lasts. As divorce is unheard of in the countryside, as it would lead to the breakup of farms, a woman only becomes (or becomes once more, if she was so prior to her marriage) head of a farm upon the death of her husband.

PASSIVE RESISTANCE VERSUS ENTHUSIASTIC COMMITMENT

In this sort of situation (where the head of the family is also head of the farm), one might expect him to play a driving role in the dewitching process and work resolutely toward finding a solution. Such, however, is not the case, as each of the dewitchings I took part in separately confirmed. He believes, of course, in witchcraft, just like most locals and is convinced he needs dewitching, and he will attend the dewitching sessions but he shows no real enthusiasm. His wife, on the other hand, displays an immediate and fervent commitment (*adhesion*) to the dewitcher's recommendations, enthusiastically cooperating in the treatment and seemingly prepared to do anything to save the family.

This differential participation of the sexes does not depend on the personality of the bewitched couple nor on the gender and personality of the dewitcher. It appears with such regularity that it suggests the following hypothesis: dewitching qua therapy specifically tailored to farming families can only achieve its goals by playing on social relations between the sexes. As the aim is to help the head of family and farm (who, in the world of farming, is always the man) reclaim and reassert his position of leadership, he is the particular object of a therapeutic process that must cure him (by enabling him to wield indirect violence) without openly calling into question his honor as a man, as a leader, as representative of family and farm in the eyes of the local and national community.

SALVATION IN THE FORM OF FEMININE WILES

The simple fact, however, of needing a dewitcher impugns his honor in at least two ways. First, the man's plea for help is made on behalf of his farm and family unit but it is nonetheless an implicit recognition of his incapacity to preserve the holding's bioeconomical potential and of the need temporarily to relinquish his statutory authority. From that moment forward, he is no longer sole master of his house: the dewitcher's recommendations are as binding as the law in a limited but vital sphere—that of protecting the farm and so ensuring its survival. And second, his role as representative of the farm and family ought normally to oblige him to adopt the official discourse of scorn for witchcraft. This official discourse has failed, however, to explain the cycle of misfortune and rational measures cannot resolve them and so he has been forced to rely on the theory of witchcraft and its practical instantiation: dewitching. He would rather, though, that nobody knew and he would even rather not know himself. This is why he consistently plays down his wife's assertions during the séance and interrupts the dewitcher to express his reticence, saying, "You mustn't believe it all" or "It's really my wife, not me, who says that."

For the wife, the situation is less awkward. The fact that she is, in principle, powerless and without responsibility means that she need not declare her incapacity to act or cede any of her power. What is more, she has no ideological honor to defend and so can happily embrace her belief in witchcraft. Indeed, this institutional recognition of the crisis actually improves her situation in two ways. First, she achieves temporary equality with her husband and master (an equality of suffering and powerlessness, a shared submission to the external authority of the dewitcher); and second, she is accorded for the first time a degree of responsibility, as she and her husband play an equal part in applying the dewitcher's recommendations. She has the right, and even a duty, to consider the best way to implement the program, the right and a duty to take the initiative, to criticize her master's supine attitude . . . in short, the right and a duty to play an active role in saving the farm. And so she enthusiastically embraces (*adhésion*) the therapy.

By the same token, it is doubly humiliating for the bewitched farmer to carry out the dewitcher's recommendations. Some of these recommendations are so clearly recognizable as belonging to the register of dewitching that they open him up to the suspicion and even scorn of the wider community, stripping him of his status as a civilized, rational, and peaceful person—e.g., the repetition of his interlocutor's last words or the act of "salting someone's ass" and "locking everything down." All these actions are unmanly ways of managing conflict and dealing with an enemy.

On top of this, some of the recommendations force him to adopt stances and styles of action that are unworthy of a man—stances and styles that society typically assigns to women. Thus, many of the recommendations are strangely reminiscent of housework, with its host of minor tasks that must constantly begin anew: cutting out little pieces of red cloth and sewing them into protective sachets for the entire family; collecting the ingredients to fill the sachets; removing and reattaching the sachets each time one changes undergarments; filling one's pockets with holy salts; placing planks full of nails and bowls of holy water with charcoal in them under the beds to protect the family while it sleeps (as well as changing the water when it evaporates); fetching supplies of holy water from outside the parish to avoid the priest's mockery; and getting medals of Saint Benedict without rousing the monks' suspicions. And the dewitcher's recommendations to the family are similar in nature to those normally recommended to women to help avoid male violence: lock oneself away, avoid unnecessary contact, don't leave oneself exposed. And where one can't avoid contact with a witch, play it cunning, try to interpret the slightest sign on their part, and engage in intense, aggressive noncommunication. In other words, engage in the sorts of indirect violence proper to the dominated and socially hampered—i.e., to women—and at the same time, obey the dewitcher implicitly, just as a wife should submit to her husband.

When crisis strikes and rattles the farm and the husband has proved helpless, so behavior and skills associated with women and normally scorned acquire a nobility, a dignity, and above all, a vital utility of their own. The women seize upon this newfound (albeit limited) autonomy and begin to assert themselves when it comes to the proper execution of the recommendations. For instance, a wife might insist, after the first sé-ance, on immediately collecting all the ingredients of magical protection rather than putting things off for the morrow. Or she might insist that prayers come before agricultural work. She may hector him if he accepts the suspected witch's outstretched hand or fails to touch the holy salts in his pockets. All bewitched people show remarkable zeal in carrying out the rituals but the initiative belongs to women, who make a point of honor of their flawless execution. This is not a challenge to the master of the house and farm but merely scrupulous obedience of the dewitcher for the good of family and farm. As a higher power (higher at least than the husband, for the time being) has commanded it, wives can cast aside their fear of being too obtrusive or demanding of their husbands.

Stunned at having to resort to such measures to reassert his role as master and startled by this series of domestic tasks imposed upon him, the husband is of course inclined to leave the greater part of ritual activity to his wife. If, for instance, he comes with her to get holy water from a church, he will often wait in the car; at best, he might keep watch. She has to fill the bottles and run the risk of being reprimanded by the priest, and it is she who does the dirty work and all the minor tasks. The husband does what he must, but it is she who supplies the labor power. This also deprives him of the psychological benefits of undertaking ritual activity. While his wife runs the gamut of subtle varieties of indirect violence and tastes the sweet fruits of efficacious activity, the head of the household does as little as possible and complains that it makes no dif-ference, without realizing that his wife's constant labor is changing her.

THERAPY AS HOUSEWORK

It will come as no surprise that wives begin to change very rapidly. Their fears and inhibitions vanish and they discover vast reserves of energy, enthu-siasm, and creativity. One might even say that after a few short weeks the wife is normally dewitched, were it not for the fact that dewitching thought denies the possibility of conceiving of her as an individual: she has no reti-cence about accusing potential witches and denouncing them in her prayers, imagining killing them, fixing them with a stony gaze when she meets them, and "salting their asses" if they come to the farm. And this self-assurance bleeds into her management of day-to-day relations and problems.

This marks the beginning of the next and longest stage: the invisible therapeutic work about the house carried out by the wife on her husband. For once she rediscovers her energy, she sets out to reignite that of her husband, helped in this task by the visits and comments of the dewitcher. Her enthusiastic application of the latter's recommendations and subsequent reaping of the benefits serves as a model for her husband. She is a living model of therapeutic success. Her constant efforts to familiarize him with indirect violence and bring him to embrace it finally win him over and draw him into the behavior recommended by the dewitcher. After a few months, the husband too happily sets out to collect the necessary magical ingredients, says his prayers of defensive aggression, spies on the witch, and fixes him/her with a stony gaze. The husband, of course, is blind to his wife's therapeutic activity and here again, she is simply engaged in the normal work of women and deploying women's skills: taking care of and supporting the family and finding a way to make them accept what is best for them. Indeed, as soon as the farm and the family have escaped the cycle of misfortune, then relations between the sexes return to that happy prior state from which they would ideally never have deviated, and the wife's determining role in the dewitching is swiftly forgotten. Family members of both sexes will later refer back to the dewitching period in terms of perfect indivision: "We set to it," "We did what needed doing."

Dewitching therapy, then, operates in two distinct phases: first, the wife is cured by direct means (as she immediately adopts and benefits from the dewitcher's proposed plan of action); and then the cure works on the husband through the wife.

This tells us something about the place of women in such farms. In farms that have not been bewitched, the wife is not joint head with the husband but a family help or chattel, awarded the prestigious but hollow title of "*patronne*" (boss). If the farm is caught up in crisis, however, she suffers alongside her husband. And if he cannot face up to the crisis, she cannot do so in his stead; she cannot assume the role of temporary head. What dewitching shows is that she can, at most, help treat him, help him to stand once more on his own two feet. She undertakes a huge effort to liberate some kind of force but all for the sake of the farm that is symbolically linked to her husband's name. The wife's therapeutic labor (which is invisible to those concerned) is an extension of her normal role and is an integral part of domestic production—she is a family help in the strictest sense of the term.

ON NOT BEING AN "INDIVIDUAL PRODUCER"

We might say that a successful dewitching requires cooperation between two therapists: an official, paid specialist (the dewitcher) and an unofficial, unpaid, and professionally unqualified family help (the wife). This cooperation between the two parties with their apparently quite different statuses poses a problem for us: what is it that unites them and contrasts them with the head of the farm who is the object of the therapy?

Let us begin with the farmers themselves. In my experience, the bewitched (and the witches) are always heads of small family firms, normally family farms, but occasionally shopkeepers or craftsmen whose professional activity depends on the unpaid labor of their wives, if not the entire family (e.g., bakers, pork butchers, grocers, seed merchants, etc.).[3] As these family firms are invariably managed by a single person, that person must be a man, as only he is culturally considered a potential "individual producer," both locally and nationally—i.e., in the Bocage, both public opinion and witching discourse see things thus, and in France as a whole, this holds for public opinion and the laws and regulations concerning family firms, as well as national accounts systems, economics (which distinguishes between heads of family or family firm ["producers"] and subordinate family members ["consumers"]), and vital records (which describe the latter as "without profession").

It is immediately clear in what consists the contrast between the farmer and his unofficial therapist: while the bewitched man is endowed with the status of "individual [i.e., family] producer," his wife/therapist

---

3. I never heard of a bewitched person belonging to one of the following social categories: inhabitant of the county town, unmarried, widowed, or divorced, pensioner, worker, employee, or civil servant, shopkeeper, or craftsman engaged in a trade that does not require family input.

has no such status. Whatever she does (whatever labor she provides, whatever services she renders to the failing farm) she is not the "producer," she is not the "individual entrepreneur." As regards the official therapist, the mere fact that many dewitchers are women demonstrates that, unlike their clients, dewitchers do not have the status of "individual producers" for their families. What is more, man or woman, one tends to become a dewitcher after a major life crisis, often a run of deaths in the family. In any case, dewitchers of both sexes tend to be relatively unencumbered by family ties. Either their family is dead or it is diminished (their partner may be dead, their children have flown the nest, or they may have set up house on their own). They cannot, however, be bachelors or spinsters. To be a dewitcher/therapist, one must previously have been caught up in family ties (marriage and children) and now partially disentangled from them.

Where dewitchers are men, their professional activity is not tied up with the existence of a family. Even if they are farmers and so are formally endowed with the status of "head of the family holding," they are nonfamilial producers because they no longer have a family; they are individual producers in the strict sense of the term. The shopkeepers and tradesmen among them work in properly individual professions where no family input is required (hairdressers, gelders, etc.). And finally, dewitching is a highly demanding profession that requires practitioners to be available around the clock, especially at night. So as a dewitcher develops a wide client base, he tends to abandon his original profession or reduce it to a shell identity protecting him from police and the taxman. Neither the new profession (dewitching) nor the original one require any family input.

In short, female therapists (both official and unofficial, dewitcher and wife), unlike bewitched men, are never endowed with the status of "individual [family] producer." Meanwhile, dewitchers who still have an official profession may either be endowed with this status de jure but not de facto, because they no longer have a family or they may be strictly individual producers who are not reliant on family input.

When a family farm is struck by a crisis that has all the hallmarks of witchcraft, it is the "individual producer" who is affected and also he who resists the cure most strongly. To help him recover (almost despite himself), his therapists must have a different social status than "individual producer," either because they never had such a status or because they abandoned or were stripped of it. It is the price that must be paid to practice dewitching, to teach the art of indirect violence to heads of families and family farms who are incapable of it.[4]

IT'S SINCE I SET UP IN MY OWN NAME . . .

Of course, the bewitched themselves do not feel that they lack anything to succeed (except the "force" that the witch has sucked from them). As regards their professional activity, the bewitched's complaint can be reduced to two declarations that all their different narratives tend to illustrate: "We've only ever had losses . . . it's since I set up in my own name." In an agricultural context, the term "losses" (*pertes*) refers indiscriminately to all the following situations: failed productivity, poor sales, running down the operating capital, losing land to some cunning competitor, et cetera. In agriculture, of course, it is neither the nature, nor the quality, nor the quantity of labor that determines a farmer's income; instead, it is sales that matter. To earn his living and, a fortiori, to succeed, a farmer needs two distinct skill sets: a producer's and an entrepreneur's. A conscientious or experienced arable or hill-farmer will labor for naught if he cannot master the vagaries of the market, if he cannot buy, sell, and haggle and manage the power relations between people, companies, and institutions. This is the case for bewitched farmers who work themselves to the bone and experience only "losses." This allows us to formulate a first hypothesis concerning what it is that dewitching therapy actually treats: as some producers are incapable of assuming the position of "force" or "aggression" necessary to entrepreneurial activity, the dewitcher guides them toward it. (In this context—that of the psycho-sociology of the family firm—we might just as well only use the term "aggressiveness").

Second, setting up in "one's own name," and acquiring the formal markers of the position of farmer and material means of exercising the profession (i.e., becoming the head of a family holding) mean being rapidly confronted by a series of perilous social challenges. In a few short

---

4.   Underlying my theory there is a clinical hypothesis: as this confusion between family and firm is pathological, one must be outside it in order to treat it.

weeks, a young man must perform a complete about-turn—one that will commit him for life (Deplhy 1974). He goes from being family help (i.e., subaltern, obedient, and dependent) to being the head of a concern. Though he may have worked for ten years on his father's farm, he received no salary and had no means of his own. To accomplish this shift in status, then, he is entirely dependent on parental largesse, his wife's dowry and so-called setting-up endowments (*donations d'établissement*): with no land of his own and without a tenancy agreement, he cannot be registered as a farmer at the Chamber of Agriculture and the mayor's office; without an operating capital, ready cash, and livestock (either dead or alive), he cannot improve his lands.

One of the particularities of farming (and this is especially the case in the Bocage, where small farms are the norm) is that a young, unmarried, and subaltern man can only become head of a family and head of a farm at the expense of all his close relatives. One becomes an "individual producer" by despoiling, eliminating, and expropriating one's immediate forebears, collateral kin, and wife, and this requires the deployment of a certain amount of violence—a violence that is quite legal and culturally acceptable but nonetheless very real. A description of a typical process of inheritance, whereby a son acquires part of his father's farm, will illustrate this.

When he becomes head of a family, the young farmer acquires a "labor-team" (i.e., unpaid assistance with no professional status) composed of first his wife and then any children as well. It is no exaggeration to say that he exploits the labor of this family help as it is he and he alone who is socially recognized as a "producer," who decides on questions of management, and can dispose of any income. The collective flight of young people and women from the world of farming demonstrates this.

A young farmer who inherits part of his father's farm and combines it with a tenancy agreement on an adjoining piece of land must spend the next thirty years (when both generations will still be working) eating away at his father's land and operating capital. Whether his father chose him or he imposed his right to be the "successor" (*reprenant*), his inheritance implies the spoliation of his brothers, who must look to set themselves up on other land and in more precarious situations. The successor does not have to look for land, he benefits from using the farm buildings and established livestock (part of which is given to him and the rest of which he buys, little by little and at an advantageous price). Between the successor and his brothers, then, there is a considerable disparity of situation that is never compensated for by the endless calculations and recalculations of gifts and inheritance. What is more, the fact that the successor is invariably male excludes unmarried women. When the inheritance is later divided up, each child receives an equal share (as the law stipulates), but the daughters only receive part of their official share, and often none whatsoever if the successor cannot free up the capital necessary to pay them off.

In short, even in a mixed-tenure region like the Bocage, where tenant farms outnumber owner-operated farms, it is still the case that once a holding has been established, it should stay in the family as long as possible. There can only be one successor, however, who manipulates social relations between the generations and between the sexes, as well as power relations with his brothers, to eliminate all possible rivals and lay claim to the lion's share of the inheritance and of family labor.

These reflections on the emergence of "individual producers" in an agricultural context allow the formulation of a second hypothesis about what it is that dewitching therapy actually treats: in agriculture and other trades or professions that depend on the fusion of family and firm, only men can be individual producers—and this by virtue of a particular liberty taken with language that is also a liberty taken with certain people. Though they are culturally authorized to practice this form of violence and are inculcated into it from the cradle onward, not all "individual producers" necessarily have the psychic wherewithal to deal with the consequences of these acts of despoilment, elimination, and direct expropriation of their relatives' inheritance. It may well be local "custom" (or part of the "symbolic order") to succeed one's father, eliminate one's brothers, and disinherit one's sisters but that does not mean that the psychic cost of such actions is null.

We can, then, draw together both the two elements of bewitched farmers' complaints and with them the two clinical hypotheses they suggest: the farmer or tradesman who is psychologically ill-equipped to perpetrate the series of acts of violence necessary to inheriting, getting married, and setting up on one's own is, a fortiori, ill-equipped to perform the aggression toward strangers and nonrelatives (i.e., economic partners) necessary to the position of entrepreneur.

A CATCH-UP INSTITUTION

If one asks local people who witches tend to be (i.e., which social category they are drawn from) the invariable answer is that they are "neighbors." If one looks more closely at specific cases, the following patterns emerge: the "neighbor" in question never lives very far away (less than three miles) but there are often several other neighbors who actually live closer by. The original nuclear families of the bewitched couple are excluded from the list of suspects, even if they happen to live in the neighborhood. Members of the extended family are only rarely accused of witchcraft and those who are, are usually kin by marriage (an uncle who is then described as an outsider—"my aunt's husband") and are only accused of petty witchcraft. Farmers only ever accuse other farmers, and shopkeepers and tradesmen only accuse their peers from the same village. This incrimination of geographical "neighbors" means that witchcraft is situated in a particular social space: neither too near (relatives) nor too far (strangers or members of other professions). Too great a geographical and social distance is, in any case, excluded by local understandings of witchcraft, which presuppose regular communication between the two parties.

My plentiful experience of the interminable negotiations surrounding the identity of the witch that occur during dewitching sessions also allows me to add the following details. For a socio-geographical "neighbor" to be identified as a witch, it is also necessary that the bewitched man not be engaged in direct hostilities with him but instead have an "intimate" (*investie*) relationship with him (a best friend is a credible suspect). At the same time, though, he must be ready to watch him suffer and even die. The geographical and social proximity of the witch are, thus, seconded by a personal proximity, and here again the parties must be neither too close nor too distant.

Finally, when the bewitched family comes to the dewitcher for the first time, they are of course familiar with witching theory ("the witch must be a neighbor") but they are still frequently convinced that the witch must be a family member (often a brother, sometimes a father). I repeatedly saw that the dewitcher is expecting this and tries, from the outset, to discourage it: even before they have mentioned any names, he will say, "The one who's doing it [the witch] isn't who you think" and he goes to great lengths to disabuse them of this conviction, ignoring their veiled references to relatives and posing repeated questions about unrelated "neighbors."

From the fifties to the seventies, Anglo-American anthropology was interested in African witchcraft accusations for what they revealed about underlying structural tensions in a given group. Natives, themselves, were held to be implicitly aware of this (Marwick 1970). People's claims that they were caught up in a witching relationship with somebody else (e.g., X accusing Y of having caused him to sicken) were false (X is indeed ill but witchcraft is not to blame), but they did reveal the existence of a real social relationship (Y might be X's usurer, cowife, or maternal uncle). These necessarily problematic relations (close, but tense) provoked conflicts that could not be resolved by the official institutional apparatus of society but could be managed via witchcraft. Native statements about witching relations were, then, simultaneously metastatements about the structural tensions proper to their society.

Even if these propositions are true of the African context, it is by no means established that all accusations of witchcraft in all societies describe those relations that are locally considered most problematic. One would need to prove that members of each of these societies make two mutually reinforcing kinds of statement: one concerning witchcraft and the other concerning social tensions. This is not something we see in the Bocage. The statement concerning witchcraft ("Here, it is neighbors who bewitch one other") is not supported by any social commentary on the especially problematic nature of neighborly relations.[5] Outside of the context of witchcraft, people's comments regarding social tensions do not stress the problematic nature of neighborliness. Instead, the focus exclusively on "family hatreds" (*les haines de famille*)—i.e., conflicts between potential successors to a farm or firm (involving brothers and, occasionally, sisters' husbands) that grow venomous when the succession is finally at stake: when a decision is taken as to who will succeed, when dowries and setting-up endowments are calculated, and when the inheritance is divided up.

---

5. Individual people's statements also reflect the wider social discourse: Bocagite witchcraft refuses to confirm Marwick's famous description of the phenomenon as a "social strain gauge."

Those British mechanics of social organization saw witchcraft as an error that couldn't help itself revealing a truth—a social relation. The Bocage case, though, suggests that though one may still consider witchcraft to be an error, it can only be thought of as revealing a decoy: Bocagites accuse their "neighbors" so as not to mention their "family hatreds." Perhaps, then, we should abandon once and for all the question of the true and the false and look at Bocagite dewitching as a "catch-up institution" (*institution de rattrapage*): one designed to help certain people (heads of family farms and farms) learn to internalize and reproduce strategies and behaviors that they have failed to acquire, unlike most of their peers, who do so without difficulty as they are legally and culturally authorized to act this way, and social inculcation of norms and rites of passage all help them on the way. And perhaps this idea of "catch-up institutions" might also be a useful way of thinking about all forms of therapy, be they "primitive" or European, rural or urban, illiterate or learned, and however they seek to justify their existence.

CHAPTER SIX

Being affected

My work on Bocage witchcraft gradually led me to reconsider the notion of affect and the importance of exploring it, both as a way of addressing a critical dimension of fieldwork (the state of being affected) and as a starting point for developing an anthropology of therapy (be it "primitive" and exotic or learned and Western). Finally, I contend that affect can be used as a way of rethinking anthropology itself.

Indeed, my efforts to challenge anthropology's paradoxical treatment of affect as a notion were inspired by my experience of fieldwork (of dewitching) and psychoanalysis (therapy). The central role of affect in human experience has frequently been neglected or denied; and when it is acknowledged, this is either (as testified to by an abundant body of Anglo-American literature) in order to demonstrate that affect is a purely cultural construction and has no reality outside of this construction, or (as testified to by French ethnology, as well as psychoanalysis), to condemn affect to irrelevancy by forcing it into the realm of representation. My work, on the contrary, focuses on the idea that the efficacy of therapy depends on an engagement with nonrepresentational forms of affect.

More generally, my work calls into question anthropology's parochial emphasis on the ideal aspects of the human experience, on the cultural production of "understanding," to employ a term derived from classical philosophy. It seems to me that there is an urgent need to rehabilitate old-fashioned "sensibility," the more so as we are now better equipped to address it than the seventeenth-century philosophers were.

First, however, a few reflections on the manner in which I obtained my field-data. I could not but be affected by witchcraft and I developed a methodological approach that subsequently allowed me to put this experience to use. This approach was neither participant observation, nor, above all, empathy.

When I went to the Bocage in 1969, there already existed an abundant literature on witchcraft, divided into two separate currents, each unaware of the other: that of the European folklorists (who had recently upgraded themselves to the status of "ethnologists," though their way of approaching the subject had remained unchanged) and that of Anglo-American anthropologists, especially Africanists and functionalists.

The European folklorists had no direct knowledge of rural witchcraft: following Van Gennep's recommendations, they conducted regional studies, meeting with local elites (the people least likely to know anything about it) or presenting them with questionnaires and then tacking on a few interviews with peasants to see if people still believed in it. The responses received were as uniform in nature as the questions: "Not here, but in the neighboring village—they're backward . . ." followed by a few skeptical anecdotes, ridiculing believers. In short, French ethnologists interested in witchcraft avoided both participation and observation—indeed, this is still largely the case today (Favret-Saada 1987).

Anglo-American anthropologists at least claimed to practice "participant observation." It took me some time to work out what they actually meant by this curious expression, in empirical terms. In rhetoric, it's called an oxymoron: observing while participating, or participating while observing—this is about as straightforward as eating a burning hot ice cream. In the field, my colleagues seemed to combine two types of behavior: an active stance, involving regular work with paid informants whom they would interrogate and observe; and a passive one, in which they attended events linked to witchcraft (disputes, visits to mediums, etc.). The first type of behavior can scarcely be described as "participation" (though the informant does indeed appear to "participate" in the ethnographer's work); and in the second case, participation seems to mean trying to be present, which is the minimum requirement for observation.

In other words, what mattered, for these anthropologists, was not participation, but observation. They had in fact a rather narrow conception of it: their analysis of witchcraft was reduced to that of accusations because, they said, those were the only "facts" an ethnographer could "observe." For them, accusation was a type of "behavior." In fact, it was the principal form of behavior present in witchcraft (its archetypal action), as it was the only one that could empirically be proven to exist. The rest was little more than native error and imagination. (Let us note in passing that, for these authors, speaking is neither a behavior nor an act capable of being observed.) These anthropologists gave clear answers to one question and one question only, "In a given society, who accuses whom of witchcraft?" and disregarded almost all the others: How does one enter into the state of being bewitched? How does one escape from it? What are the ideas, experiences, and practices of the bewitched and of witches? Even an author as precise as Turner does not help us to answer these questions and we are forced to return to the work of Evans-Pritchard (1937).

Generally speaking, the relevant literature blurred the boundaries between a number of terms that it would have been well to distinguish: "truth" overlapped with "reality," which in turn was confused with the "observable" (this term also confusing empirically attestable knowledge with that knowledge which could be accessed independently of native discourse) and then with such terms as "fact," "act," and "behavior." The only thing that united this terminological nebula was that each term could be contrasted with its symmetrical opposite: "error" overlapped with "imaginary," which in turn overlapped with "unobservable," "belief," and finally with native "discourse."

Nothing is in fact as uncertain as the status of native speech in these texts: sometimes, it is classified as a behavior (as with accusations) and sometimes as a source of false propositions (as when witchcraft is used to explain illness). The act of speech itself, however, is magicked away and native discourse is reduced to its end product—acts of speech mistaken for propositions. Symbolic activity, then, is little more than false propositions. As we see, all these confusions circle around one common point: the disqualification of native speech and the promotion of that of the ethnographer—whose activity seems to consist of making a detour through Africa in order to verify that only he holds . . . we're

not sure what, a set of vaguely related notions that, for him, apparently
equal the truth.

Let us go back to my work on witchcraft in the Bocage. As I read
the Anglo-American literature to help understand my field, I was struck
by a curious obsession present in all of the prefaces. The authors (and
the great Evans-Prichard is no exception) regularly denied the possibility of rural witchcraft in contemporary Europe: it was seemingly long
dead and buried. Mair, Evans-Pritchard, Douglas, Marwick, Thomas
(to cite just a few well-known authors) always discuss it in the past tense.[1]
Marwick is particularly explicit about this. According to him, the end
of criminal trials for witchcraft in the seventeenth century represented
our "emancipation" from widespread belief in witchcraft. The idea that
witchcraft might, in our societies, have continued to bubble along under
the surface is "debatable," a "figment of the imagination." "In modern
society," witchcraft has been reduced to "myths and fairy-tales," it has
fled to the "realm of fantasy." Those practices that today still claim to be
"witchcraft" are mere "artificial cults" and "utter fabrications." Marwick
doubtless has in mind the famous British covens, a recent urban practice
that should not, in fact, be associated with rural witchcraft (Marwick
1979: 11).[2]

However, the refusal, within Anglo-American anthropological literature, to admit the existence of rural witchcraft in Europe, was always
coupled with reflections on the distance that "we are meant to maintain with witchcraft." It lies outside our immediate experience and es-
capes our understanding. So, possessed as we are of a "European spirit,"

---

1. See Mair (1969), Evans-Pritchard (1937, 1972), Marwick (1970), Douglas
    (1970), Thomas (1971). J. Caro Baroja's book, *Les Sorcières et leur monde*
    (1972) was translated into English, but its readers do not seem to draw
    any conclusions from the few pages where he notes the presence of peasant
    witchcraft in the Basque country.

2. On these present-day urban cults, see, for example, Glass (1965). To say
    that rural witchcraft disappeared in seventeenth-century Europe is factu-
    ally false, as attested to by eighteenth-century reports detailing Episcopa-
    lian visits; in the nineteenth century, reports from prefects, certain criminal
    archives, and the work of folklorists; finally, in the twentieth century, we
    find press reports and a few European ethnographic works dedicated to
    witchcraft.

we must take a detour via exotic anthropology in order to represent it (Middleton and Winter 1963). Or it is claimed that it only exists in "small-scale societies . . . out of touch with modern science" and with "limited medical knowledge." Witchcraft being the medicine of illiterate, ignorant peoples, we Europeans, with our education and medical knowledge, have no use for it (Mair 1969: 9).[3] And so these anthropologists, supposedly practitioners of the most rigorous form of empiricism, engaged in an absurd attempt to recreate the Great Divide between "Us" and "Them" ("we" also believed in witches but that was three hundred years ago, when "we" were "them"), and thereby to protect the ethnologist, this acultural entity whose mind only contained true propositions, from contamination by his object.

Perhaps this was possible in Africa, but I was in France. Bocage peasants obstinately refused to play the Great Divide with me, as they knew full well where it would end: I would be on the side of truth (that of knowledge, science, the real, see above), and they, of ignorance. The press, television, the church, school, medicine (all these national bodies of ideological control) were ready to pillory them just as soon as an example of witchcraft went wrong and led to some tragedy. For a few days, some parcel of countryside was transformed into a hotbed of infamy: people believed in witches, accused their neighbors of witchcraft, and collectively cultivated passionate hatred for it. According to the press, the lives of these peasants were not merely insignificant, they were despicable, morally repugnant, shadowed from the light of reason, and blind even to straightforward common sense. And so, Bocage peasants protected themselves from these well-intentioned institutions by building a wall of silence that they justified with statements such as, "if you've never been 'caught' (*pris*) in it you can't speak about witchcraft," or "we can't talk to them about it."

Thus, they only spoke to me about it once they thought that I too had been "caught" in it—i.e., when uncontrollable reactions on my part

---

3.   I had a long conversation with her on the topic: faced with the empirical fact of rural witchcraft in France (with me as material witness), she immediately abandoned her initial position for that of the French folklorists. Evans-Pritchard, on the other hand, jokingly dismissed it, and I admired his 1937 monograph so much that I did not insist.

showed that I had been affected by the real (and often devastating) effects of particular words or ritual acts. Some people took me for a dewitcher and asked me to help out, while others thought I was bewitched and offered their help. Notables aside (who were happy to speak of witchcraft the better to dismiss it), nobody ever discussed these things with me because I was an ethnographer.

I, myself, wasn't quite sure whether or not I was bewitched. Of course, I never believed in a propositional sense that a witch might harm me with charms or spells, but then I doubt that the peasants did either. Rather, they asked of me that I personally (rather than scientifically) experience the real effects of the particular network of human communication that is witchcraft. In other words: they wanted me to enter into it as a partner, to stake the contours of my then existence in the process. Initially, I oscillated between these two pitfalls: if I "participated," fieldwork would become a personal activity, that is to say the opposite of work, but if I attempted to "observe," meaning keeping myself at a distance, I'd have nothing to "observe." In the first case, my scientific project was threatened, but in the second, it was ruined.

Though I didn't know, when I was in the field, what I was doing nor why, I am struck by the clarity of my methodological choices: everything happened as though I had undertaken to make "participation" an instrument of knowledge. During my meetings with the bewitched and the dewitchers, I let myself be affected, without seeking to study what they were doing nor even to understand and remember it. Once home, I wrote up a sort of chronicle of these enigmatic events (often, situations occurred that were so intensely charged that they would render me incapable of this a posteriori note taking.) This field journal, which was for a long time my only material, had two objectives.

The first was very short-term: to try to understand what they wanted from me, to find an answer to such vital questions as, "Who does this person take me for?" (a woman bewitched, a dewitcher); "What does so-and-so want from me?" (that I dewitch him . . .). And I needed to find the right answer, because next time, I'd be asked to act. In general, however, this was beyond me: the ethnographic literature on witchcraft, both French and Anglo-Saxon, did not allow me to figure the positional system that constitutes witchcraft. Instead, I discovered this system by staking my own self in the process.

The other objective was more long-term: I never accepted that what was, above all, a fascinating personal experience, would remain beyond my understanding. At the time, I wasn't sure for whom or quite why I wanted to understand. For myself? For anthropology? Or even for the greater European consciousness? But I organized my field journal so that I might make something of it later on. My notes were maniacally precise, so that one day I might rehallucinate the experience and so (because I would no longer be "caught" in it but rather "recaptured") finally understand them.

Josée Contreras and I rewrote and published parts of this journal as *Corps pour corps*. Those who have read it may perhaps have noticed that there is nothing in there to link it to the journals of Malinowski or Métraux. The field journal was for them a private space where they could finally let go, find themselves again, outside the hours of work during which they forced themselves to put on a brave face in front of the natives. In short, a space for personal recreation in the literal sense of the word. Private or subjective reflections are, to the contrary, absent from my own journal except when particular events from my personal life were evoked in conversation with my interlocutors, that is to say included in the network of witchcraft communication.

One aspect of my fieldwork experiences was all but untellable. It was so complex that it defied memorization and, in any event, it affected me too much. I am speaking of the dewitching séances that I attended either as a woman bewitched (my personal life was closely scrutinized and I was ordered to alter it), or as an onlooker, present at the behest of either client or dewitcher (I was repeatedly ordered to intervene on the spot). Initially, I took a great many notes once I got home, but this was principally done to soothe the anxiety of having to engage personally. Once I accepted the place that was assigned to me during the séances, I practically never took notes again: everything went too fast, I let situations unfold without second guessing anything, and from the first séance to the last, I understood practically nothing of what was happening. But I discreetly recorded some thirty of the roughly two hundred séances I attended, in order to constitute a body of material on which I could later work.

In order to avoid any misunderstanding, I'd like to point out that "participating" and being affected are categorically not techniques for the acquisition of knowledge via empathy, however one defines it. I shall now explore two of its principal definitions and show that neither corresponds to my experience in the field.

According to the first definition, drawn from the Encyclopedia of Psychology, empathizing consists of "experiencing by proxy the feelings, perceptions, and thoughts of another." This type of empathy, then, necessarily implies distance: it is because we are not in the place of the other that we attempt to represent or imagine what it would be like to be them—what we might feel, perceive, and think. I, however, was in the native's position, shaken by the feelings, perceptions, and thoughts that affect those who are part of the system of witchcraft. I contend that one must occupy these positions rather than merely imagine them, for the simple reason that what occurs within them is literally unimaginable—at least for an ethnographer used to working on representations. When we are in such a position, we are bombarded with specific "intensities" (let us call them affects) that generally refuse expression. This position and the intensities that come with it must therefore be experienced: it is the only way to address them.

The second conception of empathy—as *Einfühlung*, which we might translate as affective communion—instead emphasizes the immediacy of communication, the interpersonal fusion one can reach via identification with another. This idea says little of the mechanism of identification, instead stressing its result: the fact that it allows for the knowledge of another's affective states. I, on the contrary, would argue that occupying such a position in the witchcraft system in no way informs me of the affective state of another; occupying such a position affects *me*, meaning it mobilizes or modifies my own stock of images, without necessarily informing me of that of my partners. However (and this is crucial, as the type of knowledge I am aiming for hinges upon it), the mere fact of my occupying this position and being affected by it opens up the possibility of a specific form of communication: a necessarily involuntary form of communication, devoid of intentionality, and one that may or may not be verbal.

When it is verbal, this is more or less what occurs: something (I cannot say what or why), drives me to speak about, say, unrepresented affect. For example, I might say to a peasant, in echo of something he previously said to me: "Actually, I dreamed that . . ." and I'd have a hard time explaining my use of the word "actually." Or, my interlocutor might remark, a propos of nothing: "The other day, so and so said this or that to you. . . . And today, you have these zits on your face . . ." In both of these cases, the speaker implies that I have been affected. In the first example, the speaker is me, while in the second it is somebody else.

And what of nonverbal communication? What is communicated and how? We are in fact dealing with the form of immediate communication invoked by the term *Einfühlung*. However, what is communicated to me is only the intensity with which the other is affected (the young Freud spoke of a "quantum of affect," or an energetic charge). The images that, for he and he alone, are associated with this intensity escape this form of communication. I, at my end, am struck by this energetic charge in my own personal way: I might, for example, suffer a temporary blurring of vision, a quasi-hallucination, or a change in dimensional perception; or I might be overwhelmed by a sense of panic or massive anxiety. It is not necessary (and in fact not common) that this also happens to my inter-locutor: superficially, he may be completely unaffected.

Let us suppose that instead of struggling against this state, I accept it as an act of communication of something unknown. This drives me to speak, but in the manner mentioned earlier ("You know what? I dreamed that . . ."), or to hold my tongue. In such instances, if I am able to forget that I am in the field, that I have my stockpile of questions to ask, . . . if I am able to tell myself that communication (ethnographic or not; that is no longer the problem) is taking place there and then, in this unbearable and incomprehensible fashion, then I can connect to a particular form of human experience—the state of being bewitched, for instance—because I am affected by it.

When two people are affected, things pass between them that are inaccessible to the ethnographer; people speak of things that ethnogra-phers do not address; or they hold their tongues, but this too is a form of communication. By experiencing the intensities linked to such a posi-tion, it is in fact possible to notice that each one presents a specific type of objectivity: events can only occur in a certain order, one can only be affected in a certain way. As we can see, the fact that an ethnographer allows herself to be affected does not mean that she identifies with the indigenous point of view nor that her fieldwork is little more than an "ego-trip." Allowing oneself to be affected does however mean that that one risks seeing one's intellectual project disintegrate. For if this intellec-tual project is omnipresent, nothing happens. But if something happens

and the intellectual project is somehow still afloat at the end of the journey, then ethnography is possible. It has, I believe, four distinctive traits:

1) Its starting point is the recognition that ordinary ethnographic communication—i.e., verbal, voluntary, and intentional communication
   that seeks to discover the informant's system of representations—is
   among the most impoverished forms of human communication. It is
   especially inept at providing information about nonverbal and involuntary aspects of experience.

   I note in passing that when an ethnographer reminisces about
   the key moments of his time in the field, he always speaks of situations where he was not capable of engaging in this impoverished
   form of communication because he was overwhelmed by a situation
   or by his own affect or both. However, within ethnographies, these
   situations of involuntary communication, frequent as they are, are
   never analyzed as what they are: the "data" the ethnographer gleaned
   from them appear in the text but with no reference to the affective
   intensity that accompanied their transmission: and these "data" are
   treated in precisely the same way as information that emerged out
   of voluntary and intentional communication. We could in fact say
   that becoming a professional ethnographer is a matter of learning to
   disguise any particular episode of one's experience in the field as an
   act of voluntary and intentional communication aimed at discover-
   ing the informant's system of representations. I, on the other hand,
   chose to grant those situations of involuntary and nonintentional
   communication an epistemological status: my ethnography consists
   of their repeated re-experience.

2) The second distinctive trait of this ethnography is that the researcher
   must tolerate a form of split experience. Depending on the situation,
   she must either give precedence to that part of her that is affected,
   malleable, modified by the experience in the field, or to the part that
   wants to record the experience in order to understand it and to make
   it into an object of science.

3) The process of understanding is spread out in time and disjointed: in
   the instant one is most affected, one cannot recount the experience.
   In the moment when it is recounted, one cannot understand it. The
   time for analysis comes later.

4) The material collected is of a particular density and its analysis inevitably leads us to break with certain well-established scientific certitudes. Take dewitching rituals. Had I never been thus affected, had I not taken part in so many informal episodes of witchcraft, I would have accorded a central importance to the rituals: first, because as an ethnographer I am supposed to privilege symbolic analysis; and second, because standard witchcraft narratives grant them pride of place. But, having spent so much time among the betwitched and dewitchers, both within and without séances, having heard a wide variety of spontaneous conversation on witchcraft, in addition to formal representations of it, having experienced so many affects associated with certain specific instances of dewitching, having seen so many things done that were not part of the realm of ritual, I was made to understand the following:

Ritual is a means (the most spectacular but not the only one) the dewitcher uses to reveal the existence of "abnormal forces," the life and death stakes of the crisis his clients are undergoing, and the possibility of victory. But this implies setting in train a very complex therapeutic device both before and long after the ritual proper. This device can, of course, be described and understood, but only by if we are prepared to run the risk of "participating," of being affected by it. It cannot simply be "observed."

And to conclude, a word on the implicit ontology of our discipline. Empiricist anthropology presupposes, among other things, the human subject's essential transparency to himself. Yet my experience in the field (because it allowed space for nonverbal, nonintentional, and involuntary communication, for the rise and free play of affective states devoid of representation) drove me to explore a thousand aspects of the subject's essential opacity to himself. This notion is in fact as old as tragedy itself, and has been at the heart of all therapeutic literature for a century or more. It matters little what name is given to this opacity (e.g., the "unconscious"): what is important, in particular for an anthropology of therapies, is to be able to posit it, and place it at the heart of our analyses.

References

Agulhon, Maurice. 1976. "Apogée et crise de la civilisation paysanne, 1789–1914." In *Histoire de la France rurale*, vol. 3, edited by Georges Duby and Armond Wallon. Paris: Le Seuil.

Caro Baroja, Julio. (1961) 1972. *Les Sorcières et leur monde.* Paris: Gallimard.

Cholvy, Gerard, and Bernard Plongeron, eds. 1976. *La religion populaire.* Paris: Beauchesne.

Cholvy, Gerard, and Yves-Marie Hilaire. 1985. *Histoire religieuse de la France contemporaine, 1800–1880.* Toulouse: Privat.

Clifford, James, and George E. Marcus, eds. 1986. *Writing culture: The poetics and politics of ethnography.* Berkeley: University of California Press.

de Certeau, Michel, Dominique Julia, and Jacques Revel. 1970. "La beauté du mort: Le concept de culture populaire." *Politique aujourd'hui.* December: 3–23.

Delphy, Christine. 1976. "La transmission du statut à Chardonneret." *Ethnologie française* 4 (1–2).

Delumeau, Jean. 1978. *La peur en occident, XIVe–XVIIe siècle.* Paris: Fayard.

Douglas, Mary. 1970. *Witchcraft confessions and accusations.* London: Tavistock Publications.

Evans-Pritchard, Edward E. 1937. *Witchcraft, oracles and magic among the Azande.* London: Oxford University Press. (French translation. 1972. *Sorcellerie, oracles et magie chez les Azande.* Paris: Gallimard.)

Favret-Saada, Jeanne. 1977. *Les mots, la mort, les sorts: La sorcellerie dans le Bocage.* Paris: Gallimard.

——. 1980. *Deadly words: Witchcraft in the Bocage.* Translated by Catherine Cullen. Cambridge: Cambridge University Press.

——. 1987. "Les culottes Petit Bateau: Dix ans d'études de la sorcellerie en France." *Gradhiva* 3: 19–31.

——. 2009. *Désorceler.* Paris: Editions de L'Olivier.

Favret-Saada, Jeanne, and Josée Contreras. 1981. *Corps pour corps: Enquête sur la sorcellerie dans le Bocage.* Paris: Gallimard.

Fournée, Jean. 1985. "Normandie." In *La Piété populaire en France: Répertoire bibliographique*, vol. 1, edited by Bernard Plongeron and Paule Lerou. Paris: Cerf.

Frémont, Armand. 1967. *L'Élevage en Normandie: Étude géographique.* Publications de la FLSH de Caen.

Gervais, Michel, Marc Jollivet, and Yves Tavernier. 1977. "La Fin de la France paysanne de 1914 à nos jours." In *Histoire de la France rurale*, vol. 4, edited by Georges Duby and Armand Wallon. Paris: Le Seuil.

Glass, Justine. 1965. *Witchcraft.* London: Neville Spearman.

Harwood, Alan. 1977. "Puerto Rican spiritism." *Culture, Medicine, and Psychiatry* 1: 69–95 and 135–53.

Lecœur, Jules. (1883, 1887) 1979. *Esquisses du Bocage normand.* 2 vols. Saint-Pierre-de-Salerne: Gérard Monfort.

Lévi-Strauss, Claude. (1949) 1963a. "The effectiveness of symbols." In *Structural anthropology*, translated by Claire Jacobson and Brooke Grundfest Schoepf, 186–205. New York: Basic Books.

——. (1949) 1963a. "The sorcerer and his magic." In *Structural anthropology*, translated by Claire Jacobson and Brooke Grundfest Schoepf, 167–85. New York: Basic Books.

——. 1958. "Préface." In *Sorciers et jeteurs de sorts*, by Marcelle Bouteiller. Paris: Plon.

Mair, Lucy. 1969. *Witchcraft.* London: Weidenfeld & Nicholson.

Marwick, Max. 1970. *Witchcraft and sorcery.* London: Penguin Books.

Middleton, John, and Edward H. Winter, eds. 1963. *Witchcraft and sorcery in East Africa.* London: Routledge and Kegan Paul.

Muchembled, Robert. 1978. *Culture populaire et culture des élites dans la France moderne (XVe–XVIIIe siècle).* Paris: Flammarion.

————. 1979. *La Sorcière au village (XVe–XVIIe siècle)*. Paris: Julliard/Gallimard.

Obeyesekere, Gananath. 1977. "The theory and practice of psychological medicine in the Ayurvedic tradition." *Culture, Medicine, and Psychiatry* 1 (2): 155–81.

Sperber, Dan. 1982. *Le savoir des anthropologues: Trois essais*. Paris: Hermann.

Tambiah, Stanley J. 1973. "Form and meaning of magical acts: A point of view." In *Modes of thought*, edited by Ruth Finnegan and Robin Horton, 199–229. London: Londres, Faber, and Faber.

————. 1977. "The cosmological and performative significance of a Thai cult of healing through meditation." *Culture, Medicine, and Psychiatry* 1 (1): 97–132.

Thomas, Keith. 1971. *Religion and the decline of magic: Studies in popular beliefs in sixteenth and seventeenth century England*. London: Weidenfeld and Nicholson.

Weber, Eugen. (1976) 1983. *La Fin des terroirs: La modernisation de la France rurale, 1870–1914*. Paris: Fayard.

Young, Allan. 1977. "Order, analogy and efficacy in Ethiopian medical divination." *Culture, Medicine, and Psychiatry* 1 (2): 183–99.

Index

A

Affect, x, 97, 98, 102–107

B

Bewitched, x–xiii, 1–5, 8, 9, 13–16, 18, 19, 21–27, 35–37, 39, 41, 42, 48–52, 54, 55, 57, 60, 62, 68–70, 73, 74, 81–83, 85–90, 92, 93, 99, 102, 103, 105
Bewitchment, xviii, 12, 13, 15–17, 21, 23, 26, 27, 30, 37, 49; state of, x, 2, 36, 97, 99, 104, 105; techniques and rituals of, 15, 16, 34–35, 38–39, 40–44
Bocage, Bocagite, ix–xii, xiv, xviii, 1, 3–5, 13, 16, 19, 30–32, 47, 88, 91, 92, 94, 95, 97, 98, 100, 101

C

Contreras, Josée, ix, xviii, 3–5, 10, 62, 103

D

Dewitcher, xi–xiii, 1–4, 9, 10, 12–27, 33, 35, 37, 40, 43, 47–50, 52, 55–57, 59–62, 81, 83–90, 93, 102, 103, 107
Dewitching, vii, ix–xi, xiii–xv, xvii, xviii, 2–4, 12–14, 17–21, 23, 24, 26–28, 30, 33–35, 47, 48, 59, 69, 81, 83–90, 92, 93, 95, 97, 103, 107; techniques and rituals of, 9, 14, 16, 17, 18, 21, 24–26, 25–38, 39–40, 43–44, 47–80; duration of, 17, 18, 24, 26, 27; understood as a form of therapy, 10, 11–14, 18, 27, 28, 29, 44–45, 47–80
Divination (for the bewitched), 17, 21–23, 47–80

E

Evans-Pritchard, E.E., xiv, 99–101

Exemplary narratives, x, 17–21, 23,
    27, 28, 30, 33–35, 41, 44, 62;
    nineteenth century, 30, 31,
        33–44, 100;
    twentieth century, 33–44, 100
Exhortatory narratives, 21, 23, 25,
    27, 28, 34, 41

F

Family firm (craftsmen, traders,
    and farmers), xiv, 7, 12, 30, 31,
    33, 39, 44, 82, 88–90, 95
Favret-Saada, Jeanne, vii, ix–xv,
    xviii, xix, 98;
    Corps pour corps, 1981, ix, xviii,
        3–6, 103;
    Deadly words, 1983, ix, xviii,
        4–6;
    fieldwork, 1969–1972, xi, xiv, xviii,
        1, 5, 6, 39, 82, 97, 102, 103
Flora (Madame Flora), xiii, xiv,
    1–5, 47–63, 65–69, 71, 75, 80, 82
Force, xii, xiii, 2, 8–10, 12, 14–16,
    19–25, 27, 33, 34, 36, 37, 39, 40,
    42–45, 49, 55, 60, 61, 81, 85, 88,
    90

G

Good vs. Evil, x, 23, 25–27, 49–80

H

Head of the farm and head of the
    family, xii, xiii, 7, 9, 17, 21–23,
    82, 83, 86–95

J

Jakobson, Roman, 5

L

Lecœur, Jules, x, 31–35, 37–39, 42
Lenormand (Mademoiselle), 48,
    50, 51, 59, 64–80;
    Le Grand Tarot, 48, 51–60,
        64–80;
    Petit Lenormand, 50, 51, 66, 67,
        69, 70, 71, 75, 76, 78
Lévi-Strauss, Claude, 11, 29, 30

M

Mair, Lucy, 100, 101
Marwick, Max, 94, 100

N

Neighbor, xii, 7, 8, 17, 19, 22, 26, 51,
    52, 56–58, 93–95, 101

P

Possession, 9, 11, 13, 16, 19, 20, 27,
    36, 40, 42

R

Revelator, 17, 18, 23

V

van Gennep, Arnold, 98
Violence shifter, xiii, 5, 52–56, 82

W

Witch, vii, xii, xv, 3, 5, 9–12, 14–20, 22–27, 33–43, 47, 49, 51–60, 62, 65–69, 71, 73, 74, 76, 77, 79, 85–87, 90, 93, 102

Witchcraft, vii, ix–xi, xiii, xiv, xviii, 1, 4–6, 8, 9, 14–17, 19–21, 27–33, 35, 36, 38–40, 44, 45, 51, 54, 56–58, 81, 83, 84, 89, 93–95, 97–104, 107

HAU Books is committed to publishing the most distinguished texts in classic and advanced anthropological theory. The titles aim to situate ethnography as the prime heuristic of anthropology, and return it to the forefront of conceptual developments in the discipline. HAU Books is sponsored by some of the world's most distinguished anthropology departments and research institutions, and releases its titles in both print editions and open-access formats.

www.haubooks.com

Supported by

Hau-N. E. T.
Network of Ethnographic Theory

University of Aarhus – EPICENTER (DK)
University of Amsterdam (NL)
University of Bergen (NO)
Brown University (US)
California Institute of Integral Studies (US)
University of Canterbury (NZ)
University of Chicago (US)
University of Colorado Boulder Libraries (US)
CNRS – Centre d'Études Himalayennes (FR)
Cornell University (US)
University of Edinburgh (UK)
The Graduate Institute, Geneva Library (CH)
University of Helsinki (FL)
Johns Hopkins University (US)
University of Kent (UK)
Lafayette College Library (US)
Institute of Social Sciences of the University of Lisbon (PL)
University of Manchester (UK)
The University of Manchester Library (UK)
Museu Nacional – UFRJ (BR)
Norwegian Museum of Cultural History (NO)
University of Oslo (NO)
University of Oslo Library (NO)
Pontificia Universidad Católica de Chile (CL)
Princeton University (US)
University of Queensland (AU)
University of Rochester (US)
Universidad Autónoma de San Luis Potosi (MX)
University of Sydney (AU)

www.haujournal.org/haunet